"This comprehensive analysis of the impact of campaign contributions on legislative success has the great virtue of explaining complicated issues in ways that are clear to those who are fresh to the topic, while at the same time providing convincing original results that may come as a surprise to those who already know the basics of the campaign-finance literature. Indeed, it presents revealing new discoveries using statistical techniques that demonstrate the major role of financial donations to the 1999 and 2000 laws that contributed most heavily to the Great Recession of 2008, which is worth the price of admission alone. This book has to be seen as the starting point for anyone new to the issue as well as for those social scientists who aim to advance our knowledge of campaign finance as it becomes increasingly important in determining legislative outcomes."
—**G. William Domhoff**, author of *Who Rules America*

"Let this book *finally* put to rest the suggestion among some academics that money in politics does not matter. With clarity and directness, Clayton Peoples complements an important political science debate with the skill and sensitivity of sociology. The upshot is not pretty, at least for the Republic, a democracy deeply corrupted by money, and an urgent need to fix it."
—**Lawrence Lessig**, Roy L. Furman Professor of Law and Leadership, Harvard Law School, USA

The Undermining of American Democracy

The public believes that politicians in the US favor special interests over their constituents and that our political institutions have become corrupt—and they are right. A growing body of evidence shows that special interests have disproportionate sway over policy via campaign contributions and lobbying. In this book, the author presents this evidence in a logical, understandable way; he then illustrates how campaign contributions harm our economy, exacerbate inequality, and undermine our democracy. One of the most startling findings of the book is that campaign contributions led to the Financial Crisis and Great Recession. The author concludes that campaign contributions have effectively created an oligarchy in the US, and, thus, reform is needed to save our democracy. The final chapter of the book suggests a number of different reforms that could be pursued—and highlights some ways in which these reforms can be achieved.

Clayton D. Peoples, Ph.D., is a faculty member in the Sociology Department at the University of Nevada, Reno. He received his Ph.D. from The Ohio State University and was an Edmond J. Safra Lab Fellow at the Edmond J. Safra Center for Ethics at Harvard University.

The Undermining of American Democracy

How Campaign Contributions Corrupt our System and Harm Us All

Clayton D. Peoples

NEW YORK AND LONDON

First published 2020
by Routledge
52 Vanderbilt Avenue, New York, NY 10017

and by Routledge
2 Park Square, Milton Park, Abingdon, Oxon, OX14 4RN

Routledge is an imprint of the Taylor & Francis Group, an informa business

© 2020 Taylor & Francis

The right of Clayton D. Peoples to be identified as author of this work has been asserted by him in accordance with sections 77 and 78 of the Copyright, Designs and Patents Act 1988.

All rights reserved. No part of this book may be reprinted or reproduced or utilised in any form or by any electronic, mechanical, or other means, now known or hereafter invented, including photocopying and recording, or in any information storage or retrieval system, without permission in writing from the publishers.

Trademark notice: Product or corporate names may be trademarks or registered trademarks, and are used only for identification and explanation without intent to infringe.

Library of Congress Cataloging-in-Publication Data
A catalog record for this title has been requested

ISBN: 978-0-367-34276-0 (hbk)
ISBN: 978-0-367-34277-7 (pbk)
ISBN: 978-0-429-32480-2 (ebk)

Typeset in Bembo
by codeMantra

 Printed in the United Kingdom
by Henry Ling Limited

This book is dedicated first and foremost to my beloved family members, who have supported me throughout the process. It is also dedicated to those who have engaged in social action to bring about positive change in society.

Contents

List of Illustrations	xiii
Preface	xiv
Acknowledgements	xvii

1 Introduction   1

2 Campaign Finance Landscape   7
Types of Contributions Allowed in our System Today 8
A Brief History of US Campaign Finance Law 9
Current Campaign Finance Laws and Limits 11
    The Federal Election Commission 12
Contribution Patterns 13
    PAC Contributions 13
    Individual Contributions 15
    SuperPAC Contributions 16
Comparing/Contrasting Types of Contributions 17

3 What Contributions Do   20
The Exchange Perspective 21
Viewing Contributions as a Form of Exchange 22
Benefits for Recipients (Politicians) 23
    Increased Electoral Chances 23
    Increased Power/Sway within Political Bodies 25
    Increased Income outside Politics 26
Returns for Donors (PACs, etc.) 26
    Access 27
    Influence: Insights from Interviews/Statements 28
    Influence: Statistical Studies (Background) 29

x   *Contents*

Influence: Evidence from Statistical Studies 31
The Causality Question 33
Where and When Contributions Matter 34
Where 34
When 35
Who Benefits? 36
Summary of What Contributions Do 36

4   Implications for the Economy   41
The Financial Crisis of 2007–08 42
The Housing Bubble 42
Banking Industry Meltdown 43
The Great Recession of 2008–09 45
What Caused the Financial Crisis and Great Recession? 46
Regulations and Deregulation 46
Gramm-Leach-Bliley Act and Commodity
Futures Modernization Act 47
GLBA 47
CFMA 48
Campaign Contributions and the GLBA, CFMA 48
Variables and Methods 48
Findings 49
What it all Means 50

5   Implications for Social Inequality   52
Recent History of Inequality in the US 53
Measuring Inequality 53
Why Inequality Matters 55
How Campaign Contributions Increase Inequality 58
Government Contracts 59
Subsidies 60
The Tax Code 61
Adding it all Up 65

6   Implications for our Democracy   69
Democracy versus Autocracy, Oligarchy 69
Free and Fair Elections 70
Freedom of Speech 71
Access to Leaders 72
Violations of the Law 73

Contents xi

Bribery 74
   Are Contributions Bribery? 76
Organizational Deviance 77
   Violating External Norms 77
   Support within Politics 78
   Known at the Top 78
   Socializing New Members 79
Institutional Corruption 79
State-Corporate Crime 80
Main Takeaways 81

7 Implications for Theories of Power Structure   86
Three Main Theories of Power Structure 86
   Pluralist Theory 86
   Elite-Power Theory ("Class Dominance") 87
   State-Centered Theory ("Institutionalism") 89
Testing Theories of Power Structure 89
   Case Studies 90
   Empirical Research 91
      Special Interest Influence 92
      Who Wins? 93
      Summary of Empirical Results 94
Discussion 94

8 Political Reform   97
Campaign Finance Reform 97
   Transparency/Disclosure 97
   Stricter Limits 99
   Small-Dollar Financing 100
   Anonymous Contributions 100
   Public Financing 101
Other Reforms 103
   Change the Policymaking Process 103
      Single-Issue Legislation 104
      Bill Size/Number Limits 104
      Congressional Expert Office 105
   Close the Revolving Door 106
   Reduce Conflicts of Interest 107
      Strengthen the Federal Election Commission 107
      Forbid Politicians from Writing their Own Rules 108
      Fortify Ethics Committees 109

xii *Contents*

How Reform can Happen 110
    Congress 110
    The Supreme Court 111
        Free Speech versus Corruption 111
    Other Avenues of Reform 112
        State-Level Legislation 112
        Article V Convention 113
        Social Movements 113
Conclusions 114

Index   117

Illustrations

Figures

6.1 "Duke" Cunningham's list of bribe amounts he requested from clients in exchange for respective government contracts   75

Tables

2.1 Total Cost of Federal Elections, 2000–2018   13
2.2 PAC Contributions to Federal Campaigns, 2000–2018   14
2.3 Percent of Business PAC, Labor PAC, and Ideological PAC Money Going to Republicans versus Democrats in Federal Elections, 2000–2018   15

Preface

Nearly 70 percent of the general public believes that Congress favors special interests over constituents, and more than 50 percent of the public feels that Congress is corrupt (Dugan 2015). Is this true? Does Congress favor special interests over constituents? Has it become corrupt? If so, what are the ramifications for society?

Unfortunately, evidence suggests that Congress does, in fact, favor special interests over constituents. Campaign donors have a significant influence on policy (Peoples 2010), and policy therefore reflects the interests of elites rather than the public (Gilens and Page 2014). Because of the disproportionate influence of contributors on policy, Congress can be considered a corrupt institution (Lessig 2013). This has far-reaching implications for our economy, inequality, and democracy itself.

In this book, I will provide new evidence showing how campaign contributions helped lead to the Financial Crisis and Great Recession through influence on policies such as the Gramm-Leach-Bliley Act and the Commodity Futures Modernization Act. I will also illustrate how campaign contributions can create and exacerbate social inequality through, for instance, favoritism in government contracts (Hogan et al. 2006), government subsidies (Lopez 2003), and alterations in the tax code. Ultimately, I will argue that our democracy is in great jeopardy because of campaign contributions, and that the system needs to be changed.

In terms of how this book came about, I first became interested in the money-and-politics nexus in my early years as a sociology graduate student at Ohio State University. My interest led me to complete a Master's Thesis project in 2001 on how campaign contributions influence roll call votes in the Ohio Legislature. This initial work served as a foundation for further research—this time at the federal level.

Preface xv

For my doctoral dissertation, which I finished in 2005, I examined the impact of PAC donations on roll call voting in a two-year session of the US House. Unlike in the Ohio Legislature, where the impact of contributions works *through* party, I found that PAC donations influence voting *independent* of party in the US House. This significant finding spurred even more research on the role of money in politics.

After completing my dissertation, I expanded the analysis to include more sessions of Congress, ultimately examining more than 7,000 bills across sixteen years of policymaking in the House—the largest study of its kind (Peoples 2010). I also branched out to conduct an analysis of another country—Canada—to see if contributions affect policymaking there. I found that the patterns revealed in my dissertation extended to other years in the US House. Of the eight two-year sessions of Congress I examined, only one session (2001–02) failed to exhibit a significant effect of money on votes. Interestingly, the analysis of Canada did not yield a significant pattern, suggesting that money does not have the same influence in Canada's parliament as it does here (Peoples and Gortari 2008).

After conducting the above studies—and publishing around a dozen scholarly articles and/or chapters based on that research—I began to think about the potential impact of campaign contributions on our economy and our political system. This led me to conduct research at the Edmond J. Safra Center for Ethics at Harvard University where I did a study on how campaign donations played a role in the Financial Crisis and ensuing Great Recession. In my research, I found that PAC contributions influenced voting on the Gramm-Leach-Bliley Act of 1999 and the Commodity Futures Modernization Act of 2000, both of which played a significant role in bringing about the Financial Crisis. In short, campaign contributions have an adverse impact on our economy and helped spur the largest economic downturn since the Great Depression.

This book is the culmination of the above work—particularly the research I conducted at the Edmond J. Safra Center for Ethics at Harvard University. Although the book shows that campaign contributions have an adverse impact on our economy and our political system, it also offers some hope: Through campaign finance reform or other political adjustments, we can lessen the corrosive impact of money on our political system and, in turn, reduce risks to our economy and society as a whole.

xvi *Preface*

References

Dugan, Andrew. 2015. "Majority of Americans See Congress as Out of Touch, Corrupt." *Gallup*. https://news.gallup.com/poll/185918/majority-americans-congress-touch-corrupt.aspx

Gilens, Martin, and Benjamin I. Page. 2014. "Testing Theories of American Politics: Elites, Interest Groups, and Average Citizens." *Perspectives on Politics* 12:564–581.

Hogan, Michael J., Michael A. Long, and Paul B. Stretesky. 2006. "Campaign Contributions, Post-War Reconstruction Contracts, and State Crime." *Deviant Behavior* 27:269–297.

Lessig, Lawrence. 2013. "Foreword: 'Institutional Corruption' Defined." *Journal of Law, Medicine and Ethics* 41:553–555.

Lopez, Rigoberto A. 2003. "Campaign Contributions and Agricultural Subsidies." *Economics and Politics* 13:257–279. https://doi.org/10.1111/1468-0343.00093

Peoples, Clayton D. 2010. "Contributor Influence in Congress: Social Ties and PAC Effects on U.S. House Policymaking." *The Sociological Quarterly* 51:649–677.

Peoples, Clayton D. and Michael Gortari. 2008. "The Impact of Campaign Contributions on Policymaking in the U.S. and Canada: Theoretical and Public Policy Implications." *Research in Political Sociology* 17:43–64.

Acknowledgements

I wish to thank the University of Nevada, Reno and Ohio State University for providing me with research infrastructures within which I could conduct the work found within these pages. Likewise, I wish to thank the Edmond J. Safra Center for Ethics at Harvard University for providing an excellent research environment—and affiliates of the center for engaging conversations, feedback on my research, etc.

I wish to thank the following entities and grant programs for generous support that helped fund research connected to this book: the Edmond J. Safra Center for Ethics; the Dirksen Congressional Center; the Association for Canadian Studies in the US; and the Scholarly and Creative Activities Grant program at the University of Nevada, Reno.

Last but not least, I wish to thank all of the various mentors and colleagues who, over the years, have had a positive impact on me and my research. It would be impossible to include everyone in these few pages, but I am especially grateful to Kazimierz M. Slomczynski, J. Craig Jenkins, James Moody, Richard J. Lundman, G. William Domhoff, Steven H. Lopez, and Vincent J. Roscigno.

1 Introduction

The 2016 federal elections in the US were the most expensive on record: a total of $6.5billion was spent on presidential, house, and senate races combined (Center for Responsive Politics 2019a). Moreover, as a result of the *Citizens United* decision six years prior, lone donors were able to contribute tens of millions of dollars to SuperPACs in the 2016 elections. For instance, Sheldon Adelson gave over $77million, and Thomas Steyer donated a whopping $89million (Center for Responsive Politics 2019b).

The US campaign finance system is unique. Unlike other countries—where political campaigns are relatively inexpensive and are largely funded with public money—the US has very expensive campaigns that are mostly financed with private donations. Our campaign finance system allows private individuals and entities (e.g. businesses) to donate money to politicians and political organizations (e.g. SuperPACs) in copious sums. Although there are some limits on contributions, a large amount of money—totaling billions of dollars, as above—is donated each election cycle. Moreover, a very small number of individuals and entities account for the vast majority of that money (Olsen-Phillips et al. 2015).

With so much money in politics coming from a small number of private donors, there are some questions that are worth asking: Are politicians influenced by their donors when making decisions? Does policy reflect the interests of contributors rather than the interest of the general populace? If the answers to the above questions are "yes," an important follow-up question is warranted: Do these patterns have an adverse impact on society?

Looking at public opinion polls, it is clear that most Americans feel the answer to the above questions is "yes." The public believes that the current campaign finance system in the US is flawed and that political bodies, such as Congress, have become corrupt. A 2011 CBS News poll found that people believe special interests have more

2 *Introduction*

influence than ordinary citizens. A more recent poll showed that 69 percent of the population believe that Congress favors special interests over constituent concerns, and more than 50 percent believe Congress is corrupt (Dugan 2015).

Anecdotal cases of bribery and campaign finance violations in recent years seem to support the public's beliefs. Members of Congress such as Bob Ney of Ohio, James Traficant (also of Ohio), Randall "Duke" Cunningham of California, and William Jefferson of Louisiana were all involved in cases of alleged malfeasance and/or bribery—and all of them were found guilty and spent time in prison. Infamous lobbyist Jack Abramoff also pleaded guilty to corruption/conspiracy and served a prison term for his crimes. And in August of 2018, Michael Cohen, a former lawyer to President Trump, pleaded guilty to two counts of violating campaign finance laws during the 2016 election and was subsequently sentenced to three years in prison.

Although bribery cases and political wrongdoing make for interesting reading, they may not be reflective of broader patterns. Put differently, it may be that the politicians and others mentioned in the previous paragraph were just a "few bad apples" and the rest are more honorable. This was the argument forwarded by Representative Ken Calvert when some of the above scandals broke. In an interview, he said, "People should recognize that 99 percent of [lawmakers] are honest and hard-working, but unfortunately there are a few bad apples" (Barrera 2006). What is the truth?

Politicians are, indeed, influenced by their donors when making policy decisions. Although the literature on this topic was mixed prior to the 2000s, more recent studies have produced a definitive answer: contributors influence policy. Meta-analyses—statistical analysis of many studies all at once—estimate that around one in three roll call votes in Congress is influenced by political action committee (PAC) contributions (Stratmann 2005; Roscoe and Jenkins 2005). My own study of more than 7,000 votes across a sixteen-year period in Congress yields similar findings—contributions significantly sway legislative votes (Peoples 2010).

Policy reflects the interests of wealthy donors rather than the wishes of the general public. Research by Gilens and Page (2014) shows that policy more closely matches the views of the elite than the preferences of the public. This corroborates long-standing work by Domhoff (e.g. 1967, 2014), which argues that it is the wealthy upper class in the US that largely dictates policy—and, by extension, gets what it wants.

This leads us to arguably the most important question of all: Does contributor influence have an adverse impact on society? One could make the case that contributors may act as benevolent powers whose influence still benefits others in society; an alternative argument, however, is that their influence enriches them at the expense of everyone else. Unfortunately, evidence is emerging that lends support to the latter stance: contributors get what they want to the detriment of the rest of society.

I will present new evidence in this book that shows how contributors helped create the Financial Crisis and ensuing Great Recession, which cost the economy about $14trillion (Luttrell et al. 2013) and caused millions of people to lose their jobs and their homes (Institute for Policy Research 2014). There are two bills—the Gramm–Leach–Bliley Act (GLBA) of 1999 and the Commodity Futures Modernization Act (CFMA) of 2000—that led directly to the Financial Crisis. Donors wanted these acts to become law, and policymakers voted on these bills accordingly. The single greatest determinant of voting on these acts was campaign contributions. In other words, campaign donations influenced passage of the GLBA and the CFMA, which, in turn, created the conditions that brought about the Financial Crisis and the Great Recession.

I will also provide evidence in the book that illustrates how campaign contributions can create and exacerbate social inequality. Research shows that political donations can give some firms an advantage over others with respect to government contracts (Hogan et al. 2006). Additional scholarship shows that campaign contributions can result in generous subsidies for particular industries (Lopez 2003), which not only creates inequality between industries, but also takes funding away from initiatives that could help the general public. But perhaps the biggest source of inequality connected to campaign contributions is alterations in the tax code. Although the US technically has a progressive tax system, it is not nearly as progressive as it could be. The wealthy pay a far lower share of taxes in the US than they do in other countries, and corporations have been paying an ever-decreasing proportion of the total taxes collected in the US since the 1950s. Campaign contributions likely play a significant role in shaping tax policy in the US, as Clawson et al. (1998) find that PAC officers brag that tax code changes are among their most important accomplishments.

Sadly, the influence of campaign contributions on policy—and its damaging impacts on our society—suggest that our democracy is withering. Democracy refers to rule by the people, and is

4 *Introduction*

characterized by free and fair elections, freedom of speech, and easy access to one's political representatives. Elections are anything but free and fair in the US because of our campaign finance system. The candidates with the most money typically win—even controlling for things like incumbency advantage. Although we do have "freedom of speech" in the traditional sense, the reality is that our speech is typically only heard by lawmakers if accompanied by a generous campaign contribution. This means that we have only limited access to our political representatives—access that is dictated largely by money. It's essentially a "pay to play" system: if we have given a contribution, we can get the ear of Washington politicians; if we haven't provided a campaign donation, we will not be heard. Instead of being a democratic system, our government has effectively become an oligarchy.

The above patterns carry significant implications for political theory. There are three main theories that seek to explain power structure: pluralist theory, which argues that the government is open to input from a variety of groups; elite-power theory, which contends that our political system is mostly only open to elite influence; and state-centered theory, which posits that governmental actors are autonomous, impervious to outside influences. Elite power theory is best supported by the findings highlighted above. Moneyed interests and the elite have significant sway over policy and generally get what they want. The rest of society suffers for it, as does our political system itself. Clearly, some kind of reform is needed.

There are numerous options to pursue in terms of campaign finance reform, from stricter limits all the way to full public financing of political campaigns. There are also a number of other possibilities that might reduce the impact of political donations on policy. Some options include changing the policymaking process to reduce the avenues through which contributors and lobbyists can shape legislation, closing the revolving door that allows politicians to secure lucrative lobbying posts once they've left office, and reducing conflicts of interest. These reforms could be pursued via any number of paths, from traditional (e.g. Congress or the Supreme Court) to citizen-initiated (e.g. social movements such as the "Democracy for All" movement). The final chapter of the book—Chapter 8—will discuss these possibilities in much greater detail. But before that, other chapters will provide a background on campaign finance in the US and outline the many problems with our system.

Chapter 2 will provide a basic picture of the campaign finance landscape in the US by briefly discussing its history and highlighting current campaign finance laws. Chapter 3 will outline the benefits of campaign donations for the recipients (politicians), such as increased electoral chances and lucrative opportunities outside of politics (e.g. lobbying); it will also delineate the returns for the donors, such as access and policy influence. Chapter 4 will dive into the implications of contribution influence for our economy, highlighting the case of the Financial Crisis and ensuing Great Recession. In a related vein, Chapter 5 will underscore how campaign contributions impact not just our economy, but also our inequality structure through things mentioned earlier (e.g. contracts, subsidies, the tax code). Chapter 6 will then discuss the implications of contribution influence for our political system—and will argue that we have effectively become an oligarchy rather than a democracy. Chapter 7 will show how these patterns speak to the debates around power structure—and how they illustrate that elite-power theory is the best explanation of power in the US today. Finally, Chapter 8 will discuss the reform possibilities noted above.

References

Barrera, Edward. 2006. "FBI Reviews Calvert Links: Association with Lewis Unlikely to Thwart Representative's Bid for House Appropriations Seat." *San Bernardino Sun* (06/18/2006).

Center for Responsive Politics. 2019a. "Cost of Election." *OpenSecrets.* www.opensecrets.org/overview/cost.php/

Center for Responsive Politics. 2019b. "Top Individual Contributors to Super PACs." *OpenSecrets.* www.opensecrets.org/overview/topindivs. php?cycle=2016&view=sp

Clawson, Dan, Alan Neustadtl, and Mark Weller. 1998. *Dollars and Votes: How Business Campaign Contributions Subvert Democracy.* Philadelphia: Temple University Press.

Domhoff, G. William. 1967. *Who Rules America?* Englewood Cliffs, NJ: Prentice Hall.

Domhoff, G. William. 2014. *Who Rules America? The Triumph of the Corporate Rich.* 7th Ed. New York: McGraw-Hill.

Dugan, Andrew. 2015. "Majority of Americans See Congress as Out of Touch, Corrupt." *Gallup.* https://news.gallup.com/poll/185918/majority-americans-congress-touch-corrupt.aspx

Gilens, Martin, and Benjamin I. Page. 2014. "Testing Theories of American Politics: Elites, Interest Groups, and Average Citizens." *Perspectives on Politics* 12:564–581.

Hogan, Michael J., Michael A. Long, and Paul B. Stretesky. 2006. "Campaign Contributions, Post-War Reconstruction Contracts, and State Crime." *Deviant Behavior* 27:269–297.

6 Introduction

Institute for Policy Research. 2014. "The Great Recession: Over but Not Gone?" *Institute for Policy Research (IPR)*. www.ipr.northwestern.edu/about/news/2014/IPR-research-Great-Recession-unemployment-foreclosures-safety-net-fertility-public-opinion.html

Lopez, Rigoberto A. 2003. "Campaign Contributions and Agricultural Subsidies." *Economics and Politics* 13:257–279. https://doi.org/10.1111/1468-0343.00093

Luttrell, David, Tyler Atkinson and Harvey Rosenblum. 2013. "Assessing the Costs and Consequences of the 2007–09 Financial Crisis and Its Aftermath." *DallasFed*, Economic Letter. www.dallasfed.org/~/media/Documents/research/eclett/2013/el1307.ashx

Olsen-Phillips, Peter, Russ Choma, Sarah Bryner and Doug Weber. 2015. "The Political One Percent of the One Percent in 2014: Mega Donors Fuel Rising Cost of Elections." *OpenSecrets News. Center for Responsive Politics*. www.opensecrets.org/news/2015/04/the-political-one-percent-of-the-one-percent-in-2014-mega-donors-fuel-rising-cost-of-elections/

Peoples, Clayton D. 2010. "Contributor Influence in Congress: Social Ties and PAC Effects on U.S. House Policymaking." *The Sociological Quarterly* 51:649–677.

Roscoe, Douglas D. and Shannon Jenkins. 2005. "A Meta-Analysis of Campaign Contributions' Impact on Roll Call Voting." *Social Science Quarterly* 86:52–68.

Stratmann, Thomas. 2005. "Some Talk: Money in Politics: A (Partial) Review of the Literature." *Public Choice* 124:135–156.

2 Campaign Finance Landscape

The US campaign finance system allows for generous private donations to political campaigns. Although other countries also allow campaign contributions, the amount of money donated in the US—and the percent of funding coming from private sources—is staggering.

Around $6.3billion was spent on US federal elections in 2012—a record at the time; $6.5billion was spent in 2016—a new record. In most other countries, total campaign spending does not even reach $1billion, let alone $6billion. The US outpaces all other countries in campaign spending, and it appears our pace of spending will not slow anytime soon.

The vast majority of campaign money in the US comes from private sources. Although presidential candidates can access public financing if they choose to use the Presidential Election Campaign Fund (to be described in more detail in Chapter 8), the majority of candidates opt out of this system because of the restrictions it entails. Moreover, no public options exist for candidates seeking other offices (e.g. congressional candidates). In other words, private donations are the primary source of funding for political campaigns in the US—in part because the system is not structured in a way that allows for viable alternatives (e.g. public financing).

The aim of this chapter is to provide a general landscape of our campaign finance system. It will begin by briefly outlining the different types of contributions that are allowed today. It will then provide a history of campaign finance law in the US before shedding light on current laws and limits. After that, it will get into more detail, showing how much money goes to campaigns from various sources. The chapter will also identify some of the top contributors in each category to reveal who is giving the most to federal campaigns.

8 *Campaign Finance Landscape*

Types of Contributions Allowed in our System Today

In the US campaign finance system today, there are effectively two main categories of contributions allowed: direct "hard money" donations, and indirect "independent expenditures." Within each of these categories, then, there are specific types of contributions. They will be discussed below.

As the name implies, direct "hard money" donations are contributions that are given directly to the candidates from donors. Within the realm of hard money donations, there are two specific types, distinguished according to *who* the donor is: First, there are *individual contributions*, which are donations from individuals. Second, there are *Political Action Committee (PAC) contributions*, which are donations from groups ("PACs") that gather and give money on behalf of entities that are, themselves, prohibited from contributing directly to candidates (e.g. corporations, labor unions, etc.)

Unlike direct "hard money" donations, indirect "independent expenditures" cannot be given directly to candidates. Moreover, donors are barred from coordinating with a candidate or the candidate's campaign—although it is sometimes unclear exactly what is meant by "coordination." In the past, independent expenditures were known as "soft money" donations; but soft money was temporarily restricted with the passage of the 2002 Bipartisan Campaign Reform Act (BCRA—sometimes referred to as the "McCain-Feingold" reform in reference to its Senate cosponsors, John McCain and Russell Feingold). Since then, however, new forms of independent expenditures have emerged. In the 2004 and 2008 Presidential Elections, we saw the emergence of "527 Groups," so named after the tax code loophole they exploited. Then, after the *Citizens United v. Federal Election Commission* 558 US 50 Supreme Court decision in 2010 repealed much of the BCRA, we saw the rapid ascendance of a new form of independent expenditure—*SuperPAC contributions*—which have reshaped elections from 2012 into the present. Although the names we attach to independent expenditures have varied over the years (soft money, then 527 groups, now SuperPACs), their fundamental nature has remained the same in that they are difficult to track and are most prominent in presidential elections.

To summarize all of the above, there are effectively two categories of contributions in our campaign finance system—direct hard money donations and indirect independent expenditures—that result in three main types of political donations: individual contributions,

PAC contributions, and SuperPAC contributions. The following section will provide a brief history of how these different types of contributions came about—and how they have been regulated (or deregulated) in the past few decades.

A Brief History of US Campaign Finance Law

Private financing of campaigns has been a part of the US political system for a long time, dating back to the mid-1800s when presidential candidates began to solicit campaign donations, sometimes using high-pressure tactics to get people to give money. This led to one of the first laws related to campaign finance—the Naval Appropriations Bill of 1867, which prohibited candidates from soliciting money from naval workers (Center for Responsive Politics 2018a).

The first reforms targeting specific kinds of contributions came about around the turn of the century. There was some controversy over the fact that Theodore Roosevelt had received campaign contributions from corporations in his bid for the presidency. In response to public outcry, Roosevelt agreed that donations from corporations should from that point forward be banned. In his 1905 annual address to Congress, Roosevelt argued, "All contributions by corporations to any political committee or for any political purpose should be forbidden by law." Senator Benjamin Tillman of South Carolina took up the charge and introduced legislation to ban contributions from corporations and banks; it passed in 1907 and became known as the Tillman Act (Center for Responsive Politics 2018a).

In the 1930s under a different Roosevelt (Franklin D.), Congress passed a law similar to the Tillman Act—this time to restrict public utility companies from donating to political campaigns. The bill was dubbed the Public Utilities Holding Act, and was passed into law in 1935 (Center for Responsive Politics 2018a).

There was relative quiet with respect to campaign finance reform through the 1940s and 1950s, but by the late 1960s and early 1970s, there was mounting concern about the potential impact of contributions on the political process. At that time, there were few regulations restricting the amount of money donors could contribute, and disclosure was limited. These concerns led Congress to pass the Federal Election Campaign Act (FECA) in 1971.

The FECA of 1971 enacted regulations intended to monitor and limit campaign contributions. For instance, it required donors to report and disclose their campaign finance activities. It also sought to curb the growth in individual contributions, so it provided entities

10   *Campaign Finance Landscape*

more leeway in terms of pooling money from various sources and contributing it as a collective. Ironically, this allowed PACs—which had already existed, but were relatively small and powerless—to grow and flourish, leading to an explosion in PAC contributions. As such, the FECA may have curbed the growth in individual contributions, but it led to growth in PAC contributions. Nonetheless, PACs were still somewhat limited in scope with the original FECA provisions. For instance, in the original 1971 version of the FECA, the "Hatch Act provision" prohibited businesses and other entities with government contracts from creating PACs. There were also limits on *who* PACs could solicit donations from. This changed in the mid-1970s.

Partially in response to the Watergate scandal, the FECA was amended in 1974. These amendments both strengthened *and* weakened the FECA. It was strengthened in that the 1974 amendments placed stricter limits on contributions, required more detailed quarterly reporting and disclosure, and created the Federal Election Commission (FEC) to monitor campaign finance activities and ensure donors followed the law. The FECA was weakened in that the 1974 amendments removed the Hatch Act provision, thereby allowing entities with government contracts to donate to campaigns.

In 1975, an FEC "SunPAC" decision approved the use of business operating funds to solicit political money from all employees and stockholders. A 1976 decision walked this back a bit, limiting it to just stockholders and executives and their families (except for twice-yearly solicitations of other employees) but it did little to slow the growth of PACs that had begun with the FECA and subsequent decisions (Alexander 1992). Even the restrictions that emerged from the 1974 FECA amendments were weakened in the courts.

In 1976, the *Buckley v. Valeo* 424 US 1 Supreme Court case closely scrutinized the 1974 FECA amendments. The court repealed some of the amendments under concerns about limiting the "free speech" of contributors. Supreme Court decisions in subsequent decades have supported the *Buckley v. Valeo* decision, and, in some cases, have weakened the 1974 FECA amendments further. In sum, court decisions in the years following the 1974 FECA reforms "gutted much of the letter and intent of the 1970s reform efforts" (Goidel et al. 1999:27) and have led to an ever-increasing array of campaign contributions.

By the late 1990s and early 2000s, however, there was growing concern over the proliferation of soft money. There was so much concern over this shadow financing of campaigns that a bipartisan bill was passed and enacted in an effort to outlaw such donations. The BCRA of 2002 severely restricted and/or eliminated various types of soft money donations. But just like with the 1974 FECA amendments, the BCRA, too, was scrutinized by the Supreme Court in one of the most high-profile cases in recent history.

In 2010, the *Citizens United v. FEC* 558 US 310 Supreme Court decision effectively repealed parts of the BCRA—again under the umbrella of "free speech" concerns related to the First Amendment rights of donors. In so doing, it opened the floodgates to large, unregulated contributions. Along with a 2010 Court of Appeals decision—*Speechnow. org v FEC*—*Citizens United* led to the formation and proliferation of SuperPAC contributions. The *Citizens United* decision was extremely unpopular among the public, with around 80 percent of people expressing opposition to the decision (Eggen 2010). The words "Citizens United" have become synonymous with out-of-control campaign spending and unfettered corporate influence in politics. Some politicians have picked up on this oppositional sentiment and proposed bills that would reverse the impact of the *Citizens United* decision, but none have been successful thus far.

Current Campaign Finance Laws and Limits

Campaign finance laws today allow for copious amounts of money to flow to candidates. There are, nonetheless, some limits, and these limits vary by type of contributor. Individual contributors are allowed to donate up to $2,700 per candidate, per election. The "per election" piece is important, because primary elections and general elections count as two separate elections. As such, individual contributors can donate $5,200 per candidate in an election year if said candidate wins the primary and goes on to compete in the general election. Until 2014, individuals had a cap of $117,000 in total contributions per election, which limited the number of candidates to whom they could donate. But this overall cap disappeared following the *McCutcheon v FEC* 572 US __ Supreme Court decision, which argued that overall limits were unconstitutional.

PACs are allowed to contribute up to $5,000 per candidate, per election. Again, as above, this limit effectively doubles to $10,000 for candidates who win their primary races and go on to the general election. Note that PACs are allowed to donate nearly twice what individual contributors are allowed to give. This may be because, as noted earlier, PACs are organizations that bundle money from many sources, so in theory they ought to be able to give more.

12 *Campaign Finance Landscape*

On the other hand, though, this means that "special interests" (PACs) can potentially have a greater influence than individual contributors. But what PACs are able to contribute pales in comparison with what SuperPACs are allowed to do.

SuperPACs are virtually unregulated. There are currently no restrictions on how much SuperPACs can spend on elections. As noted above, the only stipulation with SuperPACs is that they cannot coordinate with a particular candidate or candidate's campaign—but they are free to spend what they want in virtually whatever form they want. Moreover, there are no limits on how much individuals can donate to SuperPACs. As will be seen in the next section, some top donors alone give tens of millions of dollars to SuperPACs.

The Federal Election Commission

The Federal Election Commission (FEC) is charged with monitoring campaign finance activities, ensuring disclosure, and pursuing anomalies or infractions. But there are a number of barriers that make it difficult for the FEC to do its job effectively.

The FEC is a six-member body whose members are appointed by the President and confirmed by the Senate. This creates a conflict of interest given that politicians such as the President and senators are unlikely to appoint/confirm individuals who are tough on campaign finance infractions. A good example is Bradley Smith, an FEC appointee who wrote a book within which he praised our current system and derided the "folly" of campaign finance reform (Smith 2001).

The FEC is funded by Congress. This again creates a conflict of interest in that some of the very individuals that the FEC is tasked with monitoring are responsible for its funding. What this means is that the FEC may be reluctant to be proactive in discovering/pursuing infractions; moreover, they are unlikely to be strict when it comes to punishing violations. In short, it may not fulfill its mission. This is exactly what a former commissioner alleged in a scathing report she authored on her way out. She lamented the "dysfunction and deadlock" in the FEC and wrote that it "is not performing the job...intended, and violators of the law are given a free pass" (Ravel 2017:1). In response, another commissioner opined, "Congress set [the FEC] up to gridlock. This agency is functioning as Congress intended" (Lichtblau 2015).

Contribution Patterns

Now that we understand the past and present of our campaign finance system in the US, it is worth looking more closely at contribution patterns and trends. One trend that is undeniable when looking at the data is that contributions have been on the increase over time. In just the past twenty years or so (spanning ten election cycles), spending on presidential elections grew from $1.4billion in the 2000 election to $2.4billion in the 2016 election (Center for Responsive Politics 2018b); congressional elections show an even greater increase from $1.6billion in the 2000 election to $5.2billion in the 2018 election. Election cycles that involve both presidential and congressional elections tend to be by far the most expensive, and they have broken spending records each of the past five rounds. Illustrating this, the 2016 election, which cost a whopping $6.5billion across all federal races, broke the previous record of $6.3billion from 2012, and was more than twice the total of $3.1billion from 2000, which itself was a record at the time. More detail can be found in Table 2.1.

PAC Contributions

There are three main types of PACs: business PACs, labor PACs, and ideological PACs. A fourth type—leadership PAC—is a bit different in that it is actually internal to the political sphere and formed by politicians, rather than external and formed by outside individuals/entities; leadership PAC will be covered in more detail in Chapter 3.

Table 2.1 Total Cost of Federal Elections, 2000–2018 (Adapted from the Center for Responsive Politics 2018b)

Election	Congressional Races	Presidential Race	Total
2018	$5.2billion	–	$5.2billion
2016	$4.1billion	$2.4billion	$6.5billion*
2014	$3.8billion	–	$3.8billion
2012	$3.7billion	$2.6billion	$6.3billion*
2010	$3.6billion	–	$3.6billion
2008	$2.5billion	$2.8billion	$5.3billion*
2006	$2.9billion	–	$2.9billion
2004	$2.2billion	$1.9billion	$4.1billion*
2002	$2.1billion		$2.1billion
2000	$1.7billion	$1.4billion	$3.1billion*

* *New Federal Election Spending Record*

14   *Campaign Finance Landscape*

Business is by far the largest type of contributor. Business PACs outspend labor PACs by a factor of about 7:1 (Center for Responsive Politics 2018c). Business PACs also outspend other types of PACs, such as ideological PACs. In short, business contributes the bulk of the money going to federal elections from PACs. Moreover, the amount of money that business PACs contribute has increased steadily over time. In the 2000 election, business PACs contributed around $192million; in 2018, they donated about $393million. Labor, on the other hand, contributes about the same amount today that they contributed in the 2000 election, and, thus, donates a smaller and smaller share of the overall PAC money going to federal races. In 2000, labor accounted for about 21 percent of the PAC money donated across federal elections; in 2016, their share was just 12 percent. See Table 2.2 for more detail.

Research shows that business PACs tend to give pragmatically. In other words, they donate to the candidate who is expected to win a race—and in close elections they contribute to both candidates. At an aggregate level, this means that business PACs tend to give similar amounts to both parties, although they show a slight preference for republicans. See Table 2.3 for more detail.

Labor PACs, on the other hand, tend to give ideologically. They donate to the candidates they feel are most ideologically aligned with the interests of workers. In most cases, this means they contribute to the democratic candidate. Consequently, at an aggregate level, labor PACs tend to give substantially more of their money to democrats than to republicans. See Table 2.3 for more detail.

As their name implies, ideological PACs also tend to donate ideologically. But ideological PACs are diverse and represent

Table 2.2 PAC Contributions to Federal Campaigns, 2000–2018 (Adapted from the Center for Responsive Politics 2018c)

Election	Business PACs	Labor PACs	Ideological PACs
2018	$393million (69%)	$67million (12%)	$108million (19%)
2016	$396million (73%)	$58million (11%)	$87million (16%)
2014	$379million (73%)	$59million (11%)	$81million (16%)
2012	$365million (72%)	$66million (13%)	$75million (15%)
2010	$310million (69%)	$70million (15%)	$70million (15%)
2008	$325million (69%)	$74million (16%)	$69million (15%)
2006	$283million (67%)	$66million (16%)	$70million (17%)
2004	$239million (67%)	$62million (17%)	$54million (15%)
2002	$200million (65%)	$60million (20%)	$44million (15%)
2000	$192million (67%)	$59million (21%)	$36million (12%)

Table 2.3 Percent of Business PAC, Labor PAC, and Ideological PAC Money Going to Republicans versus Democrats in Federal Elections, 2000–2018 (Adapted from the Center for Responsive Politics 2018c)

Election	Business PACs		Labor PACs		Ideological PACs	
	Republicans	Democrats	Republicans	Democrats	Republicans	Democrats
2018	62%	38%	14%	86%	49%	51%
2016	66%	34%	14%	86%	55%	45%
2014	62%	38%	11%	89%	55%	45%
2012	63%	37%	9%	91%	55%	45%
2010	50%	50%	7%	93%	49%	51%
2008	51%	49%	8%	92%	46%	54%
2006	65%	35%	13%	87%	60%	40%
2004	66%	34%	12%	88%	60%	40%
2002	63%	37%	10%	90%	51%	49%
2000	64%	36%	8%	92%	53%	47%

interests across the political spectrum. For instance, ideological PACs represent interests as disparate as abortion rights, gun control, and environmentalism, to name a few. Because ideological PACs are so varied, their contributions, as a whole, are fairly evenly split across the two parties. See Table 2.3 for more detail.

Individual Contributions

When looking at individual contributions, it is clear that the top contributors are wealthy individuals, many of whom have business connections. This is not surprising given the dollar amounts involved—ordinary people cannot afford to donate large sums of money to political campaigns. Indeed, less than 1 percent of the population gives even $200 or more (Center for Responsive Politics 2018d), let alone the millions of dollars contributed by the top donors. The Occupy movement talked a lot about the top 1 percent, but big donors can be thought of as the "top one percent of the one percent" (Olsen-Phillips et al. 2015).

Unlike the businesses with which individual donors are associated, individual contributors tend to follow more of an ideological approach in their giving (Burris 2001). This pattern can be seen quite clearly when looking at the top individual donors in a given election. Among the top ten donors to the 2018 federal elections, all of them were extremely ideological in their giving in that they gave *all* of their contributions exclusively to members of one party

16   *Campaign Finance Landscape*

(Center for Responsive Politics 2018e). Expanding to the top twenty, there was one individual—ranked at number seventeen—who was not purely ideological—he gave 99 percent of his contributions to republicans and 1 percent to democrats. The rest gave 100 percent of their donations to members of a single party. This ideological pattern also true of donations to SuperPACs.

SuperPAC Contributions

In their donations to SuperPACs, the top contributors give in extremely ideological ways. In fact, all of the top twenty donors in the 2018 election cycle gave 100 percent of their contributions to a single side—conservative or liberal (Center for Responsive Politics 2018f). What is perhaps more striking, though, is the large sums of money given to SuperPACs. As noted earlier, the *Citizens United* decision effectively opened the floodgates to new, virtually unregulated money—and SuperPACs are the main avenue through which these unregulated funds influence campaigns. The amounts of money are almost absurd. Rather than giving "merely" a few million dollars, top donors contribute tens of millions of dollars to SuperPACs. In fact, everyone among the top ten contributors to SuperPACs in the 2018 federal elections gave at least $10million. The three biggest contributors gave $70million, $88million, and $122million, respectively!

In examining data on individual contributions to SuperPACs in 2018 (Center for Responsive Politics 2018f), there are some very well-known individuals who appear among the top ten contributors, such as Sheldon Adelson, the Las Vegas-based casino mogul; Michael Bloomberg, founder of Bloomberg LP and former mayor of New York City; Tom Steyer, billionaire hedge-fund manager; George Soros, investor; and Jeff Bezos of Amazon.com fame (and the world's wealthiest person as of this writing). Yet there are well-known individuals who do not appear on the 2018 list, such as the Koch brothers. The Koch brothers do, however, appear on the top twenty list of donors in 2014. Moreover, the Kochs have a history of utilizing a network of political organizations that do not have to disclose their donations (Maguire 2013), and, thus, do not appear in typical data archives. This network spent nearly $400million in 2012, and originally planned to spend close to $900million in 2016 (Confessore 2015) before scaling back their efforts.

Comparing/Contrasting Types of Contributions

All three types of contributors—PACs, individuals, and SuperPACs—donate large sums of money to political campaigns. Yet the purpose of the contributions varies across type of donor. Some contributors seek primarily to influence elections, whereas others vie for influence over actual policy.

Individual contributors and SuperPACs mostly seek to influence election outcomes rather than policy. Of course, general policy trajectories are affected by election outcomes—republicans are likely to pursue certain types of policies, democrats are apt to pursue other kinds of policies. But neither individual contributors nor SuperPACs seek to *directly* influence policy outcomes. Individuals are merely that—individuals. As such, they lack the policy expertise that groups (e.g. lobbying firms) possess. SuperPACs are prohibited by law from coordinating with candidates or their campaigns—which, by extension, carries over into policy formation once a candidate wins office.

PACs hope to influence election outcomes *and* policy. This can be seen in their contribution patterns. As noted earlier, while some PACs tend to donate to specific candidates or parties (e.g. labor PACs and ideological PACs), the biggest givers—business PACs—contribute in "pragmatic" ways (e.g. to the candidate expected to win). They give pragmatically because they want to impact policy once the candidate is in office. Many PACs—especially business PACs—are tightly connected to lobbying firms. Hence, the contributing arm (the PAC) donates money, and then the lobbying arm (the firm and its lobbyists) actively seeks to sway policy. The PAC establishes the relationship and gets the "foot in the door" via the campaign donation; the lobbying firm then attempts to influence policy, frequently reminding the politician of their past support (the contributions from the PAC).

Given that PACs seek to directly impact policy, scholars tend to focus much of their attention on PACs. This is especially true in studies that attempt to examine the (possible) impact of contributions on policy. Looking at PAC contributions makes the most sense given that PAC contributions are a key part of entities' efforts to move policy in their favor. Whether seeking to influence elections, or impact policy (or both), the question is, do they succeed? The following chapter—Chapter 3—addresses this exact question.

18 *Campaign Finance Landscape*

References

Alexander, Herbert E. 1992. *Financing Politics: Money, Elections, and Political Reform.* Washington, D.C.: Congressional Quarterly Press.

Burris, Val. 2001. "The Two Faces of Capital: Corporations and Individual Capitalists as Political Actors." *American Sociological Review* 66:361–381.

Center for Responsive Politics. 2018a. "Money-in-Politics Timeline." *OpenSecrets.* www.opensecrets.org/resources/learn/timeline

Center for Responsive Politics. 2018b. "Cost of Election." *OpenSecrets.* www.opensecrets.org/overview/cost.php/

Center for Responsive Politics. 2018c. "Business-Labor-Ideology Split in PAC and Individual Donations to Candidates, Parties, Super PACs and Outside Spending Groups." *OpenSecrets.* www.opensecrets.org/overview/blio.php

Center for Responsive Politics. 2018d. "Donor Demographics." *OpenSecrets.* www.opensecrets.org/overview/donordemographics.php

Center for Responsive Politics. 2018e. "Top Individual Contributors: Hard Money, by Family." *OpenSecrets.* www.opensecrets.org/overview/topindivs.php

Center for Responsive Politics. 2018f. "Top Individual Contributors to Super PACs." *OpenSecrets.* www.opensecrets.org/overview/topindivs.php

Confessore, Nicholas. 2015. "Koch Brothers' Budget of $889 Million for 2016 Is on Par with Both Parties' Spending." *New York Times.* www.nytimes.com/2015/01/27/us/politics/kochs-plan-to-spend-900-million-on-2016-campaign.html

Eggen, Dan. 2010. "Poll: Large Majority Opposes Supreme Court's Decision on Campaign Financing." *Washington Post.* www.washingtonpost.com/wp-dyn/content/article/2010/02/17/AR2010021701151.html?noredirect=on

Goidel, Robert K., Donald A. Gross, and Todd G. Shields. 1999. *Money Matters: Consequences of Campaign Finance Reform in U.S. House Elections.* Lanham, MD: Rowman & Littlefield.

Lichtblau, Eric. 2015. "F.E.C. Can't Curb 2016 Election Abuse, Commission Chief Says." *New York Times.* www.nytimes.com/2015/05/03/us/politics/fec-cant-curb-2016-election-abuse-commission-chief-says.html

Maguire, Robert. 2013. "At Least 1 in 4 Dark Money Dollars in 2012 Had Koch Links." *OpenSecrets News. Center for Responsive Politics.* www.opensecrets.org/news/2013/12/1-in-4-dark-money-dollars-in-2012-c/

Olsen-Phillips, Peter, Russ Choma, Sarah Bryner and Doug Weber. 2015. "The Political One Percent of the One Percent in 2014: Mega Donors Fuel Rising Cost of Elections." *OpenSecrets News. Center for Responsive Politics.* www.opensecrets.org/news/2015/04/the-political-one-percent-of-the-one-percent-in-2014-mega-donors-fuel-rising-cost-of-elections/

Ravel, Ann M. 2017. "Dysfunction and Deadlock: The Enforcement Crisis at the Federal Election Commission Reveals the Unlikelihood of Draining the Swamp." *Federal Election Commission.*

Smith, Bradley A. 2001. *Unfree Speech: The Folly of Campaign Finance Reform.* Princeton, N.J.: Princeton University Press.

3 What Contributions Do

In 2003, an article published by the *Journal of Economic Perspectives* made waves in that it dismissed concerns about special interest influence in politics (Ansolabehere et al. 2003). Despite finding evidence that contributions affect about one in four bills, the authors of the article alleged that donations do not matter very much. Not surprisingly, the claims of the study went viral. Magazine articles jumped on the bandwagon and questioned the money/policy connection (e.g. Burstein 2003) and newspaper op-eds declared that campaign donations have less impact than we would believe (e.g. Brooks 2010). But the premises of the 2003 article were flawed. Additionally, evidence published since 2003 has solidly refuted the article's claims.

There are logical problems with the 2003 study that are worth noting. First, it is unclear why significant findings suggesting influence in one in four bills would be dismissed by the authors. This is akin to saying, "This food item sickens only one in every four people who consume it, so it's no big deal." Just as important, the authors fail to explain why donors continue to give increasing sums of money to campaigns.

Since campaign donations began being tracked in the mid-1970s, donations have gone up in virtually every election cycle. This has only accelerated since the *Citizens United* decision. It seems highly unlikely that contributors would throw money away on something that provides no return on investment. The fact that they are giving increasing sums over time is evidence that they must be getting *something* in return.

So what do donors get in exchange for their contributions? As this chapter will show, aside from favorable election outcomes, donors gain access to politicians and influence policy. Research published since the 2003 study shows a definitive link between campaign contributions and policy decisions (e.g. Peoples 2010; Roscoe and Jenkins 2005; Stratmann 2005). In short, campaign donations provide generous returns for donors; *contributions matter.*

The Exchange Perspective

To begin the discussion on contributions and their impact, it is important to understand the exchange perspective in sociology. The exchange perspective examines the material and nonmaterial exchanges that occur between individuals, groups, and other entities. The exchange perspective argues that most interactions involve some degree of exchange. The exchanges that occur in social interactions can range from very basic social exchanges (e.g. exchange of time for the enjoyment of a person's company) to very complex financial exchanges (e.g. exchange of monetary instruments for partial ownership of a business).

A very early insight in the exchange perspective, dating back to the work of anthropologist Marcel Mauss (2000 [1923]), is that exchange typically involves some degree of reciprocation. In other words, once given something (e.g. a gift), a person will feel compelled to give something back. Indeed, the obligation to give back when given something appears to be a nearly universal human phenomenon that has sociohistorical and religious roots. Note, for instance, the centrality of the "golden rule" ("give unto others as you would have them give unto you") in Judeo-Christian traditions. Other cultures have similar traditions that have even earlier origins. For instance, the concept of "karma" ("do good things and good will come to you; do bad things and bad will come to you") has roots in Hinduism, which pre-dates Judaism and Christianity. Some even speculate that reciprocity dates back to the early hunting/gathering days of human existence and is one of the factors—in addition to our social nature, in general—that led to our survival and success as a species (Cialdini 2001).

A more recent insight in the exchange perspective is that there are numerous types of exchanges. Indirect, or generalized, exchange is when person A gives something to person B, then person B gives something to person C, and so forth. A modern manifestation of this is the "pay it forward" initiative, wherein people are encouraged to spread happiness or good deeds to others without expecting anything in return.

Direct exchange is when person A gives something to person B, then person B gives something back to person A. There are two kinds of direct exchange: negotiated exchange and reciprocal exchange.

Negotiated exchange, as its name implies, is a type of exchange relationship in which the terms of the exchange are negotiated. In some cases, the terms are literally written down (e.g. in a contract). Whether written down or not, the key distinguishing characteristic

22 *What Contributions Do*

of negotiated exchange is that things are agreed upon ahead of time. In other words, negotiated exchange is typically a scenario in which the parties would agree, "If you give me X, I'll give you Y." Other names for negotiated exchange are "quid pro quo" and "tit for tat."

Reciprocal exchange is a form of exchange in which terms are *not* negotiated. It is a much looser kind of exchange in which returns are not promised—at best, they are simply implied or anticipated. To work, reciprocal exchange relies upon the "principle of reciprocity" described by Cialdini (2001)—when given something, most of us feel compelled to give something back. This is the foundation of the classic work by Mauss (2000 [1923]) cited earlier on gifts. It is also connected to the aforementioned golden rule. Research has shown that reciprocal exchange leads to more trust, social solidarity, and affective regard than negotiated exchange (Molm et al. 2000). This may be because of the fact that the terms are not spelled out in a contract, and, thus, one needs to place more trust, etc., in one's exchange partner in anticipation of desired returns.

A final insight worth noting about social exchange is that people typically gain something in exchange relationships (Blau 1964). They may gain financially, or they might benefit in more intrinsic ways (e.g. personal satisfaction)—but all get something out of the exchange. Indeed, if people did not gain something, there would be no reason to engage in the interaction/exchange, and the relationship would be discontinued.

Viewing Contributions as a Form of Exchange

The exchange perspective is an apt lens through which to view campaign contributions and the complex relationships surrounding them. On the most basic level, the insights of Mauss (2000 [1923]) are relevant: once given a campaign contribution, the recipient (e.g. lawmaker, governor, etc.) will feel compelled to give something back.

Scholars from a number of different fields have begun to think of contributions as part of a reciprocal relationship. For instance, a well-known psychologist, Robert Cialdini, used campaign contributions as an example of the "principle of reciprocity" in his seminal work on social influence (Cialdini 2001). Political scientist Stacy Gordon highlighted reciprocity in her study of contribution influence (Gordon 2005). Finally, a team of sociological scholars—Dan Clawson, Alan Neustadtl, and Mark Weller—underscored the importance of reciprocity when looking at campaign contributions (Clawson et al. 1998).

The distinction between negotiated exchange and reciprocal exchange is also helpful when thinking about contributions. It stands to reason that most of the exchanges between contributors and politicians are reciprocal exchanges rather than negotiated exchanges. A big reason why is because negotiated exchange in this context would technically be illegal. The *Federal Bribery Statute* makes it clear that negotiated exchanges where returns are promised would qualify as bribery and are prohibited; Supreme Court opinions have upheld this standard. As such, politicians are unlikely to make explicit promises in connection with contributions.

Finally, Blau's (1964) insights are also relevant: both contributors and politicians gain from campaign contributions. The logical foundation for such a claim is pretty straightforward: Because there is no law compelling contributors to donate funds to political campaigns, the fact that they continue to give—indeed, in increasing amounts—suggests that they are gaining something from their donations. Likewise, since there are no laws forcing politicians to solicit donations, the fact that they do so—indeed, by some estimates spending the majority of their time doing so (Lessig 2011)—suggests that they, too, are gaining from contributions.

Benefits for Recipients (Politicians)

Increased Electoral Chances

Perhaps the most straightforward thing a politician gains from campaign contributions is increased electoral odds. There is a strong correlation between contributions and electoral victory: candidates with more money (relative to their opponents) are significantly more likely to win election. Some would contend, however, that this relationship may be due to incumbency advantage (Milyo 1997).

Incumbents tend to win elections. Given that some contributors (e.g. business PACs) follow a pragmatic approach when donating to campaigns—they tend to give to the favorites—more campaign money flows to incumbents than to challengers. But attributing the contribution-electoral correlation to incumbency advantage alone is a short-sighted view for a few reasons: (1) not all elections involve an incumbent, (2) money influences the trajectory of elections long before the pool is whittled down to a final list of candidates, and (3) independent of incumbency, money allows candidates to do more of what they need to do to court voters.

24   *What Contributions Do*

Although many elections involve an incumbent, some races involve an "open seat" in which there is no incumbent (e.g. the person holding the position retired or accepted a different role). Even in these races, the candidate with more campaign money tends to win. This raises serious questions about incumbency advantage being the primary driver behind the contribution-election correlation. Granted, one could argue that some of the same mechanisms—contributors donating to the candidate most likely to win—still apply in open seat elections; but contributions nonetheless come before the election, so there must be some causal relationship at play. Moreover, even if money flows to candidates who are viewed as more likely to win, receiving money helps their odds—in short, it becomes a self-fulfilling prophecy in that those viewed as safer bets receive more money, which, in turn, increases their electoral odds.

Long before a primary election and the general election there is what some refer to as the "money primary" (Goff 2004). During this invisible primary, the pool of possible candidates is narrowed. One of the key factors determining who stays and who goes in this early vetting stage is fundraising ability. Those who are able to secure the support of donors are more likely to stay in the pool; those who are not tend to fall out. Why? First, political parties favor candidates who can help the party accumulate a solid reserve of contributions. Second, it takes money to wage a successful campaign—the things that help a candidate successfully court voters all cost money, as will be described shortly. What this means is that looking at the final candidates in a general election misses the impact of money at earlier stages in the process. It is very likely that the few remaining candidates in a general election are there in part because they received more money in early phases.

Running for political office is no easy task. To persuade voters to vote for you and get them to the polls requires a multifaceted approach. You need to reach voters through advertisements, events, door-to-door canvassing, etc.—all of which costs money. Advertisements cost money—and generally speaking, the further the "reach" (more potential clicks/views), the more money it costs. Super Bowl ads are a good example: A thirty-second ad during the Super Bowl costs about $5million because it is sure to reach tens of millions of viewers (Carroll 2018). Although politicians are unlikely to advertise during the Super Bowl given that it is in February when few elections occur, the same logic applies to advertising the rest of the year—advertisements cost more the more people they reach. Mailings, lawn signs, bumper stickers, canvassing—these things all cost money as well. Political consultants and polling/analytics cost money. *Everything* one needs to wage a successful campaign costs money. This is likely part of the reason why politicians spend the majority their time in office fundraising (Lessig 2011)—and why virtually no candidates for President forgo private financing to accept the limited public funds that are available for presidential campaigns (note: an exception was John McCain in 2008, who accepted public financing—and then lost the election).

Increased Power/Sway within Political Bodies

Increased electoral chances are not the only benefit of campaign contributions for politicians. An additional advantage of contributions for politicians is sway with their colleagues. Those politicians with large amounts of money in their campaign war chest are better able to distribute money to their fellow politicians in times of need (e.g. in a close election). They are able to do this via "leadership PACs." Through leadership PACs, politicians can themselves give money to other politicians. This "gift" of money would likely compel the recipients to support the giver's causes or otherwise "return the favor" in the future, a la Mauss's (2000 [1923]) insights into gift exchanges. One example of how this might occur is co-sponsorship of legislation.

When a bill is introduced in the House or Senate, it has sponsors—lawmakers who express support for the bill and are willing to put their names on it as "authors." Fowler (2006) shows that co-sponsorship networks in the House and Senate are rich, and position in these networks illustrates influence and/or centrality in those networks. Given that campaign contributions are also related to bill co-sponsorship (Zhang and Tanger 2017), it stands to reason that the flow of money among and between lawmakers may result in expressions of support for one another's causes via co-sponsorship of legislation.

Sway with one's colleagues can translate into greater power within political bodies. Although there are many factors that determine membership on important committees or leadership positions, one factor is a person's ability to fundraise—both in the traditional sense and via leadership PACs. As the Center for Responsive Politics puts it, "ambitious lawmakers can use their leadership PACs to gain clout among their colleagues and boost their bids for leadership posts or committee chairmanships" (Center for Responsive Politics 2018). This, in turn, increases their fundraising prowess, as money often follows power. It is a self-reinforcing cycle. Recent evidence bears this out:

26   *What Contributions Do*

As of late spring 2018, the two most powerful members of Congress—the top leaders of the controlling party (republican) in the House—had the largest leadership PACs. The largest was affiliated with (outgoing) Speaker of the House Paul Ryan, with funds totaling $1.76million; the next largest was affiliated with House Majority Leader Kevin McCarthy, and had funds nearing $1.18million; after these two, leadership PACs were much smaller, with amounts well below $1millon each (Center for Responsive Politics 2018).

Increased Income outside Politics

Lastly, contributions can aid a politician achieving upward mobility outside of politics. The more money one receives as a politician, the better positioned they are for lucrative lobbying jobs—it is a classic instance of "the revolving door." This is especially true for those whose contributions led to key committee posts and leadership positions. Receiving lots of contributions and serving in important posts is a demonstration of one's connectedness. This connectedness is considered central to one's ability to lobby the government and wield policy influence.

Take, for instance, the case of Tom Daschle, a former democratic leader in the Senate from South Dakota. He lost in a stunning defeat in his 2004 re-election bid. Although the loss probably stung for a short while, he was able to quickly turn his former power in the Senate into well-paying jobs outside of government. For instance, it was reported that in 2008 Daschle earned more than $2million as a senior advisor for the law firm Alston and Bird and an additional $2million from the private equity firm InterMedia Advisors (Connolly 2009)—much better than the mid-$100,000s he earned yearly as a lawmaker. Those millions of dollars he was able to fetch as an advisor/consultant were likely a result of the value of the connections he was able to build while in a leadership position in the Senate.

Returns for Donors (PACs, etc.)

On the most basic level, contributions can help elect politicians whose views on issues align with contributors. This, however, is a very limited view of the impact of contributions. As noted in Chapter 2, some contributors—particularly business PACs—follow a "pragmatic" strategy in their giving rather than an ideological approach (Burris 2001). In other words, they donate to those expected to win a race—or both candidates in a close race—regardless of party affiliation or ideological positions. In so doing, donors are effectively "hedging their bets," thereby increasing the likelihood that they have given to the candidate who ultimately wins office. What are the rewards that come from having given to the person who wins office? They are manifold, and range from simple "access" to policy influence.

Access

The idea that contributions can lead to access is not new. Contributors and politicians alike admit as much. For instance, a corporate executive interviewed about the subject confessed, "[Without the PAC] I wouldn't have the *access*, and it may sound like [a lie], but I am telling you very sincerely, I wouldn't know...Bob Y, the local congressman as well as we know him..." (Clawson et al. 1998:78; emphasis added here). A former member of Congress provides more detail, saying, "You get invited to a dinner somewhere and someone gives you some money. And then you get a call a month later and he wants to see you. Are you going to say no? You're not going to say no. *So it does buy access*" (Schram 1995:62; emphasis added here).

More recently, a candid statement about access by a former member of Congress raised eyebrows. Mick Mulvaney, Interim Director of the Consumer Financial Protection Bureau and former congressman from South Carolina, encouraged banking industry executives to donate money to lawmakers and press their agenda, admitting, "We had a hierarchy in my office in Congress: If you're a lobbyist who never gave us money, I didn't talk to you. If you're a lobbyist who gave us money, I might talk to you" (Thrush 2018). His comments were swiftly decried as representative of "pay to play" schemes; it also appears that he was encouraging influence-peddling. But do contributions really lead to influence?

Uncovering policy influence is tricky. Obviously, the notion of contribution influence carries some controversy and elicits considerable debate. Part of the reason for this is due to the fact that influence brings one dangerously close to breaking the law. This leads some politicians (and contributors) to deny, deny, deny. For instance, one politician provided a fierce denial of influence when interviewed about contributors: "But don't ever try to create the impression with me, or ever say it—if you say it, it's all over—that your money has bought you something. It hasn't." (Jackson 1988:105). Another former lawmaker put it more simply: "There's not tit for tat in this business, no check for a vote" (Schram 1995:16). At the same time, though, some contributors and politicians will admit that contributions have an influence.

28 *What Contributions Do*

Influence: Insights from Interviews/Statements

Lawmakers sometimes admit that contributions have an influence. In certain cases, this is on specific pieces of legislation; in others, it is in a more general way. For instance, one former lawmaker suggests that the vote to provide China a "most favored nation" (MFN) trading partner status had a lot to do with campaign contributions from businesses seeking to profit from the Chinese connection:

> There's no way in hell that MFN would have passed...if all these companies hadn't come flooding in and making campaign contributions and asking for peoples' support....I know what drove that debate every year was the allure of corporate dollars flooding into members' bank accounts. *There's absolutely no doubt in my mind that money changed votes.*
>
> (Makinson 2003:66; emphasis added here)

Concerning policymaking, more generally, a former lawmaker admits, "You see the effectiveness of money in too much of the legislative process.... In some instances, the hand of the oil companies is much involved in certain amendments, or [other groups]" (Schram 1995:19). Another former lawmaker goes further, stating:

> the current method of campaign funding that we currently have...has a serious and profound impact on not only the issues that are considered in Congress, but also the outcome of those issues.... Often an issue would never have been raised in the first place were it not for the strength of a particular interest group.... And the outcome of some votes...*are influenced by the contributions* of those interests.
>
> (Schram 1995:31, 49; emphasis added here)

In a few rare instances, lawmakers will even admit to being influenced themselves. For instance, one former member confesses,

> I am sure that on many occasions—I'm not proud of it—I made the choice that I needed this big corporate client and therefore I voted for, or sponsored, its provision, even though I did not think that it was in the best interests of the country or the economy.
>
> (Schram 1995:28)

Donors also sometimes admit that their contributions get them something. Some interesting statements to this effect have come from members of the Trump administration. For instance, Betsy DeVos, Education Secretary, once said with reference to her own donations (prior to serving as Education Secretary): "I have decided to stop taking offense at the suggestion that we are buying influence. Now I simply concede the point. They are right. We do expect something in return" (as quoted in Mayer 2016). President Trump himself admitted to as much on national television during a republican primary debate: "I give to everybody. When they call, I give. And you know what? When I need something from them, two years later, three years later, I call them, and they are there for me" (as quoted in Ornitz and Struyk 2015).

So by some lawmakers' and donors' own accounts, campaign contributions sometimes influence policy. But a few politicians and contributors claiming that there is influence does not mean that there is necessarily widespread influence. Uncovering widespread influence can only be done with statistical studies and large amounts of data. But when conducting studies on this topic, researchers need to decide what type of contributions to focus on, what stage of the policymaking process to examine, and what specific statistical techniques to employ. Many have chosen to examine the influence of PAC contributions on roll call voting (the final stage of the policymaking process) via an analytical technique called regression.

Influence: Statistical Studies (Background)

Researchers frequently choose to look at PAC contributors for reasons outlined in Chapter 2. PACs seek to influence policy, whereas individuals and SuperPACs tend to focus on elections. PACs give pragmatically to help ensure access to politicians once they have won office, and PACs are often linked very closely with lobbying firms. One additional factor that makes PACs interesting to examine is that they are effectively the donating apparatuses of interest groups. Given that they solicit money around certain interests (e.g. business interests, labor interests, etc.), they are the moneyed manifestation of "special interests."

Scholars often examine the final stage of policymaking, roll call voting. The steps in passing (or rejecting) legislation are as follows: First there is agenda setting, when lawmakers decide what sorts of issues they wish to address in that particular two-year legislative cycle, rank priorities, and set goals. Next is the introduction

30 *What Contributions Do*

and cosponsoring of bills. After introduction, bills are assigned to relevant committees for discussion, revision, etc., which is when provisions can be inserted into bills; it is also a stage during which bills can "die" if they do not have enough support. Following rounds of revision/discussion in committees, bills come to the floor for a vote. If a bill passes, it goes to the other chamber (e.g. from the House to the Senate) where it is assigned to a committee, discussed/revised, and goes to a vote there. Then the two versions—one from the House, one from the Senate—are ironed out during "concurrence" before receiving a final roll call vote. After the final vote, it goes to the President, who can either approve or veto the bill.

There are many reasons why scholars tend to focus on roll call votes rather than earlier stages. One of the biggest reasons is that roll call votes are easy to access. Roll call votes become part of the public record, whereas earlier processes (e.g. agenda setting, committee discussions) often occur in private. Another reason why roll call votes are chosen by researchers for analysis is that they are readily quantifiable. To conduct statistical analyses, quantitative data are required. It is easy to convert votes into quantitative information (e.g. "yea" = 1, "nay" = 0). In a related vein, another reason why roll call votes are an attractive choice is that there are many, many votes cast in a given two-year session of Congress. Although the number of bills has fallen in recent years—for instance, there were more than 900 bills in 1948 versus around half of that by 2006 (Beam 2009)—there are still hundreds of votes cast per two-year session of Congress, which means that roll call votes provide lots data points to analyze.

With all of these data to analyze, the final question for scholars is what type of analytical technique to use. Researchers typically use regression to assess the impact of PACs on roll call votes. Regression is a kind of correlational analysis that allows one to test the impact of multiple independent (cause) variables on a single dependent (effect) variable. Granted, it is imperfect in certain ways. For instance, given that it is correlational—and correlation does not equal causation—researchers often have to perform additional analyses to increase their confidence that the findings are, in fact, causal (this will be discussed shortly). Nevertheless, regression provides researchers with the tools necessary to determine whether or not a relationship between two variables is statistically significant (due to a real association rather than chance). This makes it perfect for determining whether or not there is truly a widespread influence of contributions on policy, or if the anecdotal examples from interviews and statements are merely that—anecdotes.

Influence: Evidence from Statistical Studies

So what does the evidence show from statistical studies on the topic? There is a growing consensus today that *contributions, do, indeed, impact policy*. But there wasn't always such a strong consensus. The early literature on the topic produced disparate findings. In perhaps the most comprehensive literature review on the topic, Baumgartner and Leech (1998) found that among thirty-three studies of PAC influence on roll call voting, fourteen show significant PAC impact on voting, thirteen show marginal influence, and six show no effect at all. Unfortunately, the mixed findings led some to prematurely conclude that PACs do not influence roll call votes.

As noted in the introduction to this chapter, there were high profile claims in both the scholarly literature (Ansolabehere et al. 2003) and more popular outlets such as newspapers (Brooks 2010) and magazines (Burstein 2003) that contributions do not matter. But what these naysayers failed to acknowledge was that there were a number of problems with these early studies that accounted for their divergent results. Moreover, they did not foresee the wave of studies in 2005–2010 that would show very convincingly that PAC contributions influence votes.

One major problem in the aforementioned mixed literature is that many of the studies looked at a small number of votes—in many cases, just a single bill—and tried to generalize to all bills. But there is a significant issue with this: as noted earlier, lawmakers vote on literally hundreds of bills per two-year cycle of lawmaking. A vote on a single issue or bill—or even a few issues/bills—would not be indicative of any overall pattern. It is not surprising, then, that the studies were so mixed.

Another major problem with these early studies is that they tended to look at the effect of PACs as an atomized process occurring in a vacuum. In other words, rather than attempting to measure the social process of lawmaking, they tended to model the PAC/vote relationship as one in which a lawmaker sits alone and weighs contributions against personal ideology when making a decision. But we know that lawmakers talk with one another about decisions on bills; they also establish relationships with their contributors that some describe as "friendship." For instance, a PAC officer explained in an interview, "It's hard to quantify what is social and what is business.... Some of those [legislators] are my best *friends* on the Hill. I see them personally, socially...*they always help me with issues*" (Clawson et al. 1998:86–87, emphasis added here). Add to this the fact that

32   What Contributions Do

contributions are inextricably linked with lobbying, it is clear that contribution influence should be viewed as a social process rather than an atomized one, and that Congress should be measured as a social network.

Despite the aforementioned challenges with existing research on PAC influence, there are enough studies out there—thirty-plus—that it is possible to do meta-analyses to determine if there is at least some kind of pattern emerging in the seemingly mixed literature. A meta-analysis compiles data from a number of studies into a single analysis to establish the overall trend in an area of scholarship. Two studies in the mid-2000s did just that and came to the same conclusion: contributions influence policy.

A meta-analysis conducted by Stratmann (2005) shows that PACs significantly impact roll call voting. In the article, Stratmann writes, "This meta-analysis reverses the finding reported in existing studies that campaign contributions have no effect on legislative voting behavior. The meta-analysis performed here suggests that money does indeed influence votes" (p. 146). A meta-analysis performed by Roscoe and Jenkins (2005) shows exactly the same thing: a significant influence of contributions. In their summary of their findings, they contend that "a reasonable conclusion is that one in three roll call votes exhibits the impact of campaign contributions" (p. 64).

Although the meta-analyses described above help demonstrate a pattern in the extant literature, there are still some issues to be addressed. Namely, as noted already, studies in the literature tend to examine a small selection of bills and fail to model policymaking as a social process. To address these issues, I conducted the largest study of PAC influence done to date and published the results in *The Sociological Quarterly* in 2010 (Peoples 2010). In that study, I examined voting on all of the bills across a sixteen-year period in the US House spanning eight separate two-year Houses. I also measured policymaking as a social process in that I treated the House as a social network and looked at all possible pairs of lawmakers at the units. In so doing, I was able to treat their contributions—and their voting—as socially interdependent relationships.

The results from the 2010 study are quite telling: There was evidence of PAC influence on voting in seven of the eight Houses examined. The only House that did not exhibit evidence of influence was the 107th House (2001–02), which was when the Bipartisan Campaign Finance Reform Act (BCRA; sometimes referred to as the "McCain-Feingold Bill") was debated and passed into law. Although it is difficult to know for sure why there was no significant influence during this particular House, it seems plausible that lawmakers are more likely to behave when the public is paying attention. When the public does not care, politicians feel free to do as they wish. This fits with what politicians have said about this pattern. One former lawmaker told Martin Schram that if the public understands an issue, a donor cannot get what it wants (Schram 1995). It is also consistent with the research of Jones and Keiser (1987), who find that donor influence is *greater* on low-visibility bills than high-visibility legislation.

The Causality Question

The results from the aforementioned meta-analyses—plus my own work on sixteen years' worth of policymaking—show clearly that PAC contributions are significantly related to roll call voting. By extension, these finding strongly suggest that contributions influence policy. But what about causality? One can reasonably question whether or not a relationship between campaign contributions and voting on bills is truly evidence of a causal relationship. After all, it might be that contributions go toward lawmakers who already agree with a contributor. In short, it might *not* be that votes are the result of money; instead, it may be that money is the result of votes.

Different scholars have taken different approaches to addressing the causality question. Some scholars have used a technique called "variable replacement" within regression (Berry 1984). Variable replacement proceeds in two stages: in the first stage, the researcher constructs a variable as a substitute for the original "questionable" variable; in the second stage, the scholar runs a model with the replacement variable and assesses results.

Although variable replacement has its benefits, I have used a different strategy in my research. Knowing that causal claims hinge largely on temporality (X came before Y), I have pursued a three-pronged approach to establish causality in the contribution-vote relationship, in that (1) I have always modeled analyses such that contributions precede votes; (2) I run separate analyses for freshmen lawmakers, who have no voting history; and (3) I run additional, separate analyses on all other lawmakers—controlling for prior voting behavior.

What is the verdict? Both techniques—variable replacement and the three-pronged approach—have yielded evidence of a causal

34   *What Contributions Do*

relationship whereby contributions lead to votes. For instance, in the meta-analysis of Roscoe and Jenkins (2005), which tested models using variable replacement, they contend that "It is simply not true that the apparent connection between money and voting is just [votes causing contributions]" (p. 63). Instead, they argue, contributions cause votes. In my own work, I find that freshmen lawmakers exhibit a significant propensity toward being influenced by their contributors (Peoples 2010). Again, this is important in that freshmen lawmakers have no voting history—at least not in the US House—on which contributors could have based their contributions. I also find that non-freshmen lawmakers are influenced by their contributors, controlling for their prior voting (Peoples 2010). Including a control variable for these lawmakers' prior voting patterns is important in that it reduces the risk that any significant relationship found is due to contributors simply giving to lawmakers who already vote in their favor.

In sum, the naysayers of the early 2000s concerning the contribution/policy connection were proven wrong in subsequent years. Campaign contributions are correlated with lawmakers' votes on policy. Moreover, evidence suggests that the relationship is causal whereby contributions influence votes. As such, it is high time to put the debates to rest: *contributions do, indeed, influence policy.* But this revelation leads to an important set of follow-up questions: under what circumstances to contributions matter most, and to whose benefit

Where and When Contributions Matter

Where

We know that contributions matter in the US House. Do they matter elsewhere or in other levels of government? Evidence from outside the US is rather sparse. I conducted a study comparing the US with Canada and found that contributions have little impact in Canada (Peoples and Gortari 2008). It may be that Canada's parliamentary system affords contributors less influence than our "winner takes all" system. Very little is known about other countries, other than that contributions are given in far smaller sums than here (see discussion at the beginning of Chapter 2).

At the Federal level within the US, most research has focused on the US House; there has been little/no research done on the US Senate. This is likely because the Senate holds elections every six years on a staggered basis rather than every two, so it is more complicated to trace the impact of contributions. Likewise, there has been relatively little work on how contributions may influence the decisions of the President. One complication is the fact that the President is a single individual rather than a group. As such, options for statistical analyses are far more limited. Additionally—and importantly—the President typically does not "make" policy. Certainly, there are executive actions that effectively set policy, but the President is typically not engaged in policymaking, per se.

Evidence from different states within the US is mixed—and understandably so. States vary considerably in terms of their size—both population-wise and in terms of their economies. States also vary in the extent to which their legislatures are "professionalized" (Squire 2007). Some states, like California, have large, highly professionalized legislatures that meet regularly, get paid well for their roles, and operate much like the US Congress. Other states have smaller legislatures that meet far less frequently and offer lawmakers rather paltry pay. Evidence from California suggests that contributions influence policy in the Golden State (Gordon 2005). But evidence from Ohio suggests that contributions may only have an impact *through* party rather than directly in the Buckeye State (Peoples 2008).

When

In a general sense, studies suggest that contribution influence may be most likely to occur when the public is paying least attention. My own research over a sixteen-year period in the US House shows that the one session in which contributions did not significantly affect voting was when the BCRA was debated/passed—in other words, when campaign finance was a major national issue in the public eye (Peoples 2010). Additional research lends support to this idea. As mentioned earlier, Jones and Keiser (1987) show that contributions have the greatest impact on what they term "low visibility" bills.

Although research tends to focus on the final stage of policymaking for reasons outlined earlier, it could be that contributions have an impact on stages that come well before roll call voting—or even things outside the policy arena altogether (e.g. contracts, subsidies, etc.). Hall and Wayman (1990) suggest that contributors have a great influence at the committee level. They write, "our analysis provides solid support for the importance of moneyed interests in [earlier

36 *What Contributions Do*

stages of] the legislative process" (p. 797). Godwin and Seldon (2002) take it a step further and argue that contributors sometimes seek to influence things outside the policy realm. In their study of what businesses seek from government, they contend that a corporate lobbyist is likely to ask lawmakers "for help in obtaining government contracts, regulatory waivers, and government subsidies for the lobbyist's corporation" (p. 205), and argue that what businesses want is the "public provision of private goods" (p. 205).

Who Benefits?

As noted earlier, contributors gain many benefits from their contributions, ranging from access to policy influence. But not all contributors are equal in this respect. Research shows, for instance, that business PACs have a significant influence on policy, but labor PACs are far less consistent in their impact (Peoples 2009). This research will be described in more detail in Chapter 7, and its implications for theories of power structure will be discussed. Suffice it to say, though, it shows that some categories of contributors wield more influence than others—and big business has the most sway. Not surprisingly, research shows that big businesses and elites get what they want, policy-wise (Gilens and Page 2014).

Gilens and Page (2014) conducted a study of policies enacted by the US Congress and the extent to which these policies align with different groups' policy preferences. In particular, they looked at the policy preferences of contributors and elites versus the wishes of the general public. What they found is not shocking, but is nonetheless telling: policies tend to align with the policy preferences of donors/elites rather than the wants of the general public. The implications of this research will be discussed further in later chapters—especially Chapter 7—but it is safe to say here that their findings suggest that donors benefit from their contributions—likely at the expense of the public.

Summary of What Contributions Do

Contributions are given in huge sums—and are on the increase. There are no laws compelling donors to give money, yet they continue to do so. As such, it is safe to assume contributions provide benefits to both the recipients and the donors. What sorts of benefits come from campaign contributions? For those receiving the donations (politicians), advantages include increased electoral odds, greater power within political bodies, and enhanced opportunities for lucrative lobbying jobs once one's career in public service has ended. For those on the giving end (contributors), there are a number of things gained. Most importantly, though, is influence on policy.

There was not always a scholarly consensus surrounding the impact of contributions on policy. Through the early 2000s, research findings were mixed. This led some to prematurely conclude that contributions did not have much impact on policy. But between 2005 and 2010, a number of critical studies were done that showed convincingly that PAC contributions significantly influence roll call voting. The first of these studies were a pair of meta-analyses conducted in 2005, both of which showed that, when taken as a whole, existing scholarship does, indeed, show a significant effect of donations on policy. The other study was one conducted on over 7,000 bills over a sixteen-year span. It, too, showed a significant impact of contributions on policy. Importantly, all three of these studies addressed causality concerns and found that the causal direction is such that contributions lead to policy decisions. Given these recent findings, it is safe to conclude that contributions influence policy. Any claims to the contrary at this point would be unsupported.

The next question is when contributions matter—and to whose benefit. The answer that seems to be emerging is that contributions matter most when the public is not paying attention—and business donors benefit the most. Contributions had no significant effect on policymaking when the BCRA was debated/passed (Peoples 2010); moreover, contributions seem to have the greatest impact on "low visibility" bills (Jones and Keiser 1987). Business PACs have far greater influence on policy than labor PACs (e.g. Peoples 2009). Consequently, corporations and elites see their preferences well represented in policies that are passed and enacted, while the general public's views are largely ignored (Gilens and Page 2014).

Chapters 4 and 5 will delve more deeply into what big businesses and elites get from their contributions. These chapters will focus on the economic impact of their donations—both for the donors themselves and for society as a whole. The following two chapters—Chapters 6 and 7—will address the implication of contributor influence for our political system and theories of power structure. The final chapter—Chapter 8—will discuss ways in which we can change the system and accomplish reform.

38 *What Contributions Do*

References

Ansolabehere, Stephen, John M. de Figueiredo, and James M. Snyder, Jr. 2003. "Why is There so Little Money in U.S. Politics?" *Journal of Economic Perspectives* 17:105–130.

Baumgartner, Frank R. and Beth L. Leech. 1998. *Basic Interests: The Importance of Groups in Politics and in Political Science*. Princeton, NJ: Princeton University Press.

Beam, Christopher. 2009. "Paper Weight: The Health Care Bill is More than 1,000 Pages. Is that a Lot?" *Slate*. www.slate.com/articles/news_and_politics/explainer/2009/08/paper_weight.html

Berry, William Dale. 1984. *Nonrecursive Causal Models*. Thousand Oaks, CA: Sage Publications.

Blau, Peter M. 1964. *Exchange and Power in Social Life*. New York: Wiley.

Brooks, David. 2010. "Don't Follow the Money." *New York Times*. www.nytimes.com/2010/10/19/opinion/19brooks.html

Burris, Val. 2001. "The Two Faces of Capital: Corporations and Individual Capitalists as Political Actors." *American Sociological Review* 66:361–381.

Burstein, Paul. 2003. "Is Congress Really for Sale?" *Contexts: Understanding People in their Social Worlds* 2(3):19–25.

Carroll, Charlotte. 2018. "Super Bowl LII: How Much Does an Commercial Cost?" *Sports Illustrated*. www.si.com/nfl/2018/01/11/super-bowl-lii-ad-cost

Center for Responsive Politics. 2018. "Leadership PACs." *OpenSecrets*. www.opensecrets.org/pacs/industry.php?txt=Q03

Cialdini, Robert B. 2001. *Influence: Science and Practice*. 4th Ed. Needham Heights, MA: Allyn & Bacon.

Clawson, Dan, Alan Neustadtl, and Mark Weller. 1998. *Dollars and Votes: How Business Campaign Contributions Subvert Democracy*. Philadelphia: Temple University Press.

Connolly, Ceci. 2009. "Daschle Pays $100k in Back Taxes over Car Travel." *The Washington Post*. http://voices.washingtonpost.com/44/2009/01/30/daschle_pays_100k_in_back_taxe.html

Fowler, James H. 2006. "Legislative Cosponsorship Networks in the US House and Senate," *Social Networks* 28:454–465. https://doi.org/10.1016/j.socnet.2005.11.003.

Gilens, Martin, and Benjamin I. Page. 2014. "Testing Theories of American Politics: Elites, Interest Groups, and Average Citizens." *Perspectives on Politics* 12: 564–581.

Godwin, R. Kenneth, and Barry J. Seldon. 2002. "What Corporations Really Want from Government: The Public Provision of Private Goods." Pp. 205–224 in *Interest Group Politics*, 6th Ed., edited by Allan J. Cigler and Burdett A. Loomis. Washington, D.C.: Congressional Quarterly Press.

Goff, Michael J. 2004. *The Money Primary: The New Politics of the Early Presidential Nomination Process*. Lanham, MD: Rowman & Littlefield.

Gordon, Stacy. 2005. *Campaign Contributions and Legislative Voting Behavior: A New Approach*. New York: Routledge.

Hall, Richard L., and Frank W. Wayman. 1990. "Buying Time: Moneyed Interests and the Mobilization of Bias in Congressional Committees." *American Political Science Review* 84:797–820.

Jackson, Brooks. 1988. *Honest Graft: Big Money and the American Political Process*. New York: Knopf.

Jones, Woodrow, Jr., and K. Robert Keiser. 1987. "Issue Visibility and the Effects of PAC Money." *Social Science Quarterly* 68:170–176.

Lessig, Lawrence. 2011. *Republic, Lost: How Money Corrupts Congress—and a Plan to Stop It*. New York: Twelve.

Makinson, Larry. 2003. *Speaking Freely: Washington Insiders Talk About Money in Politics*. 2nd Ed. Washington, D.C.: Center for Responsive Politics.

Mauss, Marcel. 2000 (1923). *The Gift: The Form and Reason for Exchange in Archaic Societies*. New York: W. W. Norton.

Mayer, Jane. 2016. "Betsy DeVos, Trump's Big-Donor Education Secretary." *The New Yorker*. www.newyorker.com/news/news-desk/betsy-devos-trumps-big-donor-education-secretary

Milyo, Jeff. 1997. "Money Walks: Why Campaign Contributions Aren't as Corrupting as You Think." *Reason*. https://reason.com/1997/07/01/money-walks/

Molm, Linda D., Nobuyuki Takahashi, and Gretchen Peterson. 2000. "Risk and Trust in Social Exchange: An Experimental Test of a Classical Proposition." *American Journal of Sociology* 105:1396–1427.

Ornitz, Jill and Ryan Struyk. 2015. "Donald Trump's Surprisingly Honest Lessons about Big Money in Politics." *ABC News*. https://abcnews.go.com/Politics/donald-trumps-surprisingly-honest-lessons-big-money-politics/story?id=32993736

Peoples, Clayton D. 2008. "Uncovering Political Influence by Using Network Analyses and Exploring Contribution/Party Interactions: The Case of Ohio Legislative Voting." *Sociological Focus* 41:301–318.

Peoples, Clayton D. 2009. "Reviving Power Structure Research: Present Problems, their Solutions, and Future Directions." *Political Power and Social Theory* 20:3–38.

Peoples, Clayton D. 2010. "Contributor Influence in Congress: Social Ties and PAC Effects on U.S. House Policymaking." *The Sociological Quarterly* 51:649–677.

Peoples, Clayton D. and Michael Gortari. 2008. "The Impact of Campaign Contributions on Policymaking in the U.S. and Canada: Theoretical and Public Policy Implications." *Research in Political Sociology* 17:43–64.

Roscoe, Douglas D., and Shannon Jenkins. 2005. "A Meta-Analysis of Campaign Contributions' Impact on Roll Call Voting." *Social Science Quarterly* 86:52–68.

40 What Contributions Do

Schram, Martin. 1995. *Speaking Freely: Former Members of Congress Talk about Money in Politics*. Washington, D.C.: Center for Responsive Politics.

Squire, Peverill. 2007. "Measuring Legislative Professionalism: The Squire Index Revisited." *State Policy and Politics Quarterly* 7:211–227.

Stratmann, Thomas. 2005. "Some Talk: Money in Politics. A (Partial) Review of the Literature." *Public Choice* 124:135–156.

Thrush, Glenn. 2018. "Mulvaney, Watchdog Bureau's Leader, Advises Bankers on Ways to Curtail Agency." *New York Times*. www.nytimes.com/2018/04/24/us/mulvaney-consumer-financial-protection-bureau.html

Zhang, Daowei and Tanger, Shaun. 2017. "Is there a Connection between Campaign Contributions and Legislative Commitment? An Empirical Analysis on the Cosponsorship Activity of the 2007 Tree Act." *Forest Policy and Economics* 85:85–94. https://doi.org/10.1016/j.forpol.2017.09.007.

4 Implications for the Economy

As Chapter 3 shows very clearly, campaign contributions matter greatly for policy decisions. But the debate over campaign donations and their importance may not be entirely over. Despite the fact that contributions influence policy, there are some who would contend that campaign contributions still have minimal impact on society. After all, research by Jones and Keiser (1987) suggests that contributions matter most on low-visibility issues.

Statements from former lawmakers seem to corroborate the research of Jones and Keiser (1987). For example, one former House member interviewed by Schram (1995) notes, "The public will often look for...the grand-slam example of influence of these interests. But rarely will you find it. But you can find a million singles...regulatory change, banking committee legislation, [etc.]..." (pp. 93–94). Another former lawmaker explains why: "If the public understands the issue at any level, then special interest groups are not able to [get] an outcome that the public may not want...[but] if nobody else cares about it very much, the special interest will get its way" (p. 93).

But does low visibility equate to low impact? I would argue that it does not. The public may neither know—nor care—about certain regulations or codes, but these regulations may have an extremely significant impact on our society. Moreover, it is sometimes unclear what exactly a piece of legislation is even about. Legislation is often lengthy—in some cases, more than 1,000 pages long—and written in legalese that only lawmakers and attorneys can decipher. Plus, bills are often a hodgepodge of many, many provisions that are unrelated to the expressed purpose of the bill. In short, just because legislation is "low visibility" does not mean it is unimportant. This was certainly true of two bills passed in 1999 and 2000, respectively.

In 1999 the Gramm-Leach-Bliley Act (GLBA) was passed into law; a year later in 2000, the Commodity Futures Modernization Act (CFMA) also passed and became law. Both of these acts appeared

42   *Implications for the Economy*

on the surface to be mundane regulatory changes related to the banking industry and financial products. They were supported by a majority of lawmakers and were approved without great controversy or fanfare. But the consensus today is that these acts contributed significantly to the Financial Crisis of 2007–08 and the resultant Great Recession of 2008–09. The GLBA and CFMA were clearly of great consequence despite being low-visibility bills.

In this chapter, never-before-published evidence will be presented that links campaign contributions with the passage of the GLBA and CFMA. Not only did donors want these acts, their contributions were the single most important factor influencing lawmaker votes on the bills. As such, the evidence presented in this chapter suggests that campaign contributions *do* have a profound impact on society—and contributed to the greatest economic downturn since the Great Depression. In short, contributions matter for our economy.

The Financial Crisis of 2007–08

The Financial Crisis of 2007–08 involved failures in two major, connected parts of the economy: the housing market and the banking industry. A bubble in the housing market burst, leading to mortgage defaults and a precipitous drop in home values. Banks and related institutions that had high exposure to home loans—either as lenders or as insurers of mortgage-linked assets—incurred huge losses and faced a liquidity crisis. Some long-standing firms even went out of business. These events will be discussed further in the paragraphs below.

The Housing Bubble

In the years leading up to the Financial Crisis, an increasing number of people purchased homes in the US. This increased demand relative to supply and drove home prices skyward, creating a bubble. The reason why greater numbers of people bought homes in the lead-up to the Crisis were manifold. One factor that led to a ballooning number of homebuyers was an increasing willingness on the part of lenders to loan money to high-risk borrowers (e.g. people with low credit scores). After all, mass defaults on home loans had been a "black swan," historically—a rare event that had essentially never been seen—so lenders were willing to lend to "risky" borrowers (e.g. those with low credit scores) under the assumption they wouldn't default. A second factor that led to an increasing number of homebuyers was that many loans were negotiated via mortgage brokers rather than traditional avenues such as through loan officers at a bank. The problem with this is that mortgage brokers were paid for connecting the lender and the borrower rather than based on the long-term success of the loan. In other words, perverse incentives were in place that rewarded short-term ends rather than long-term outcomes. Credit-worthiness mattered less than simply landing someone a loan.

In a similar vein, another factor that came into play was the practice of talking borrowers into risky, adjustable-rate mortgages to get them approved for a loan. Adjustable-rate mortgages were often portrayed to prospective borrowers as a "good deal" that would allow them to afford a pricier home while they gained financial footing by starting them off at a low, teaser rate. The problem, though, is that once the low-rate term ended—typically after five or seven years—a much higher rate would kick in. One idea that was presented to borrowers at the time of signing is that they could renegotiate their loans and refinance at a fixed rate before the higher, adjustable rate kicked in. The issue with this, however, is that as the Financial Crisis unfolded, many lending institutions were unwilling to work with borrowers and refinance their loans. Combined with the fact that the Great Recession led to pay cuts and/or job loss for many people, large numbers of borrowers could no longer afford to pay their mortgages and were forced to default. This was clearly devastating for borrowers who lost their homes, but it also created major problems for the banking industry—problems that eventually spread to the rest of the economy.

Banking Industry Meltdown

As more and more borrowers defaulted on their home loans, the housing bubble began to burst. The supply and demand equation shifted 180 degrees. Before the bubble burst, demand was high relative to supply, which led to rising home prices. But as the bubble burst and more people defaulted, the supply of homes became far greater than the demand, which led to plummeting home values. From the pre-crisis peak in summer of 2006 to the bottom of the market in early 2012, home prices dropped around 35 percent nationally. In some especially hard-hit markets in states like Florida and Nevada, home values fell more than 50 percent.

Many banks were heavily exposed to the losses in the housing market and had difficulty balancing their books and ensuring liquidity. They were exposed to the losses in both traditional ways and *new* ways (largely of their own making). In a traditional sense, banks

44   *Implications for the Economy*

that had lots of home loans on their books were exposed to the cascading effects of defaults. As more and more borrowers defaulted on their loans, banks were receiving fewer interest payments—and were stuck with houses that were worth less than they had lent to the borrowers in the first place. This led to huge losses on the books. But this was only part of the problem.

In the early 2000s, banks greatly increased their leverage—the debt-to-equity ratio—from 12:1 to 30:1 or higher. This was partly due to a change in the "Net Capital Rule" in 2004, which allowed banks to take on more debt. Of course, allowing banks to do so is not the same as requiring them to do so; in other words, banks that increased their leverage did so of their own volition. That said, it led to a virtual liquidity crisis as defaults rose: banks that had a high debt-to-equity ratio—and had many borrowers default—were at great risk of not having enough money to cover withdrawal requests should depositors ask for their money (for instance, if there were a "run on the banks").

Yet another issue the banks faced—one that was far more complex than even the first two—was that many institutions were greatly exposed to risky debt-based assets and derivatives connected to home loans. In 2000, a law was passed (to be described later) that allowed for the virtually unregulated sales and swaps of derivatives such as collateralized debt obligations (CDOs). These derivatives were essentially mortgage-linked bonds that were bundled and sold, re-bundled, sold again, etc.—all of which were "insured" with credit default swaps, which, too, were swapped/sold. In essence, what emerged was a largely unregulated—and highly risky—market for the buying and selling of what turned out to be junk bonds. As the "black swan" event unfolded and people began defaulting on their home loans, these bonds dramatically fell in value and became virtually worthless.

Some banks, which by this time had combined investing with more traditional activities due to the passage of another law (to be discussed shortly), got heavily involved in the derivatives market. Those banks and other firms that had lots of derivatives or credit default swaps on their balance sheets suddenly found themselves in serious trouble. Long-standing firms such as Bear Stearns, Merrill Lynch, and Lehman Brothers faced the risk of shutting their doors. Indeed, that is exactly what happened with Lehman Brothers—they were in too deep with credit default swaps and filed for bankruptcy, closing their doors in 2008. (The other two firms, though distressed, survived—in part because they were taken over by larger firms.)

The closure of Lehman Brothers shook US and global markets. Short-term lending ground to a halt, which jeopardized liquidity in financial markets. The stock market responded with a sell-off, and stock prices tumbled. The closure of Lehman Brothers and ensuing events brought on the onset of the Great Recession.

The Great Recession of 2008–09

The Great Recession of 2008–09 is so named because of its scale—it was the largest economic downturn since the Great Depression. As the housing market collapsed and the banking industry seized up, economic growth ground to a halt. Lending slowed to a trickle, and spending decreased. These effects snowballed and led to a full-blown economic recession, defined as at least two consecutive quarters of decline in GDP. This happened in the US and lasted for approximately eighteen months (early 2008 through the summer of 2009). But the effects of the Great Recession lasted far longer than just eighteen months.

Upwards of $14trillion in value was lost during the Great Recession (Luttrell et al. 2013), and the value of assets have struggled to come back up to pre-recession levels. For instance, the stock market hit bottom in March of 2009. At that point, the DJIA had fallen to $6,443 from a pre-recession high in 2007 of $14,165. It didn't return to pre-recession levels until early 2013—approximately six years after its highs in 2007. Other assets have been even slower to recover. For instance, home prices still haven't come back up to their pre-recession highs. As of 2017, only a third of US homes had recovered to pre-recession levels, and estimates suggest it could be until 2025 before home prices have fully recovered in the vast majority of US housing markets (Riquier 2017). This is important, because for many people aside from the extremely wealthy, their house makes up a significant portion of their net worth. This speaks to a broader reality connected with the Great Recession: ordinary people have suffered the most.

As will be elucidated in Chapter 5, the rich actually saw their net worth *go up* relative to others during and after the Great Recession. Meanwhile, ordinary people have faced extreme hardship. Estimates suggest that around 4 million homes were foreclosed each year during the Great Recession, and around 8 million people lost their jobs (Institute for Policy Research 2014). Moreover, according to the US Census, the poverty rate in the US rose to around 15 percent during the recession, and has remained relatively high

46   *Implications for the Economy*

since then. Likewise, according to the US Bureau of Labor Statistics, the unemployment rate rose to 10 percent during the recession, and stayed at or above 8 percent through early 2013. In short, millions of people lost their jobs, their homes, and their livelihoods during the Great Recession; and the recovery process has been slow, with many still living at or below poverty today.

What Caused the Financial Crisis and Great Recession?

All of the events described in the previous sections played a role in bringing about the Financial Crisis and ensuing Great Recession. But what was the root cause? No one single factor bears the entirety of the blame, but deregulation was likely a significant factor. In particular, weakening of existing laws through the passage of the Gramm–Leach–Bliley Act (GLBA) and the Commodity Futures Modernization Act (CFMA) opened the door to the practices that brought the economy down.

Regulations and Deregulation

Regulations are important because they help ensure fair and stable markets and transparency in practices; they can also ensure that all businesses in a particular industry are playing by the same rules, which protects both the businesses and those impacted by the industry (e.g. consumers, the public). In short, regulations help protect everyone by providing a standard set of rules and promoting fair exchange. When regulations are weakened through deregulation, these protections go away—and the results can be catastrophic. Deregulation weakens laws that protect businesses, consumers, and the public against unfair practices, price gouging, and other forms of corporate malfeasance. This is what happened in the lead-up to the Financial Crisis. Laws that had been on the books for decades were weakened or wiped away via the GLBA and the CFMA, which meant that the people and the economy were no longer protected.

During the Great Depression that began in 1929 and carried into the 1930s, a number of regulations were put into place in an effort to prevent another severe downturn from happening in the future. One of the most important regulations was the Glass–Steagall Act. The Glass–Steagall Act was a collection of four main provisions in a larger banking bill passed in 1933, and these provisions placed regulations on the banking industry. Its most important provision concerned commercial banking (traditional, e.g. deposits, lending) versus investment banking (e.g. engaging in securities investing and trading, etc.). The Glass-Steagall Act prohibited commercial banks from engaging in investment banking and vice versa. In short, the act separated commercial and investment banking to ensure that banks did not become too large—and, perhaps more importantly, that banks did not risk depositor's monies in risky markets.

Over the years, regulatory entities began to interpret the Glass-Steagall Act's provisions more loosely. Additionally, firms began to test the boundaries of the act. For instance, Citibank merged with Travelers Group and Salomon Smith Barney to form Citigroup in the 1990s, which effectively combined commercial and investment activities. But it wasn't until the passage of two key pieces of legislation—the Gramm-Leach-Bliley Act (GLBA) in 1999 and the Commodity Futures Modernization Act (CFMA) in 2000—that portions of the Glass-Steagall Act were officially eliminated.

Gramm-Leach-Bliley Act and Commodity Futures Modernization Act

GLBA

The GLBA significantly reduced regulations on banks and their activities. It repealed portions of the Glass-Steagall Act—particularly provisions dealing with the separation of commercial banking from investing. For instance, Title I of the GLBA allowed banks to merge with entities that buy and sell securities. (Given that Citigroup had formed prior to the GLBA's introduction and passage, some refer to the act as the "Citigroup Relief Act.").

The GLBA had a number of consequences. First, it allowed for the creation of firms that were "too big to fail." Granted, some of these firms had already formed prior to the act's passage (see, e.g., the note about Citigroup, above); but the GLBA made the formation of large, blended firms officially legal. A second consequence of the act is that it increased risk by allowing traditional banks to merge with investing firms. Economist and former Chair of the Council of Economic Advisors Joseph Stiglitz said, "As a result [of the act], the culture of investment banks was conveyed to commercial banks and everyone got involved in the high-risk gambling mentality" (Baram 2008). In short, the GLBA contributed to two factors that were key to the Financial Crisis: "too big to fail" and ballooning risk.

CFMA

The CFMA deregulated the sale of certain securities and swaps. For instance, Title III of the act paved the way for transfers of financial risk via derivatives such as CDOs and credit default swaps—the very same financial instruments that firms like Lehman Brothers were too exposed to. In other words, the CFMA—and the activities it allowed—led rather directly to the events that roiled markets and brought on the Financial Crisis (and, by extension, the Great Recession).

It is clear that the GLBA and the CFMA were key contributors to the Financial Crisis and the ensuing Great Recession. Had these acts not been introduced and passed, the provisions of the Glass-Steagall Act would have still been in place—and the unregulated creation, sale, and insuring of risky derivatives such as CDOs would likely not have occurred. It could very well be that the Financial Crisis and Great Recession would not have happened without these acts. But what made the GLBA and the CFMA possible? They had the backing of campaign donors.

Campaign Contributions and the GLBA, CFMA

Banking donors wanted to see the GLBA and CFMA become law. In examining contributions from the banking industry and seeing how those contributions lined up with votes on the GLBA, the Center for Responsive Politics reports that members of Congress who voted in favor of the act received about twice the money from banking donors as those who voted against it. In specific terms, "Lawmakers voting 'yea' received about $180,000 [per person] in campaign contributions from individuals and PACs in the financial sector during [the two years leading up to the vote]. Those who voted 'nay' received about $90,000 each" (Ritsch 2008). This is a nice initial assessment of the possible impact of campaign donations on the GLBA, but we cannot be sure that there is a genuine connection between contributions and voting without running statistical analyses. Moreover, the report does not include a similar assessment of the CFMA.

Variables and Methods

To fill the above gaps, I conducted a statistical analysis of factors that influenced US House voting on the GLBA and the CFMA. Specifically, I ran a regression model for each act (the GLBA and

CFMA). In both regression models, the dependent (effect) variable was lawmaker voting; the main independent (cause) variable was PAC contributions; and statistical control variables were included for factors such as party and lawmaker demographics.

Before running the regression models, I organized data such that the units were all possible pairs of lawmakers. I did this to help account for the fact that lawmaking is a social process and, thus, the decisions of lawmakers—such as their voting on the GLBA and CFMA—are socially interdependent. In shifting the units to dyadic pairs, it changed the nature of the variables slightly. For instance, the dependent variable—lawmaker voting—was a measure of whether or not a pair of lawmakers voted the same way (both "yea" or both "nay") rather than how they voted, per se. Likewise, the main independent variable—PAC contributions—was a measure of the number of PAC contributors a pair of lawmakers shared in common rather than how many contributors they had in general. Finally, statistical control variables measured whether or not lawmakers were the same in a given respect (e.g. same party, same ethnicity) rather than their simple demographics/affiliations.

Although shifting the units to dyadic pairs of lawmakers is the best way to account for the social nature of lawmaking, it adds a minor complication in that it violates the case independence assumption of regression. Additionally, it exponentially increases the number of "cases" in the analysis (435 members times 434, divided by two). Consequently, traditional ways of determining statistical significance would be inadequate, as all variables would likely appear to be significant. To address this issue, I chose a very conservative method of determining statistical significance—quadratic assignment procedure (QAP)—that has been used by top scholars in the field (e.g. Burris 2005; Mizruchi 1992).

Findings

After running QAP regression models for both acts, I found that campaign contributions had a statistically significant influence on *both* the GLBA and the CFMA. The more donors pairs of lawmakers shared in common, the more likely they were to vote with one another (e.g. both "yea") on these bills. The effect was statistically significant at the.01 level for both acts, meaning that there is less than a 1 percent chance that the finding is due to error or other random factors. Instead, there is a greater than 99 percent chance that donors influenced lawmakers' votes on these issues.

50   *Implications for the Economy*

An important thing to note about the findings is that the effect of PAC contributors was significant even when party affiliation and other control variables were included in the models. Party is widely considered the most important predictor of lawmaker voting, yet party had very little effect on these bills. Instead, campaign donations were the most significant factor—by a large margin. No other variable even came close. As such, on both the GLBA and the CFMA, donations were the main driver behind congressional voting—even superseding the ordinarily strong effect of party.

These findings carry significant implications for our understanding of what caused the Financial Crisis and ensuing Great Recession. If we assume that the GLBA and the CFMA were instrumental in allowing the activities that led to the crisis and recession, the fact that campaign contributions were the single biggest factor predicting votes on these bills is a monumental finding. It is probably not a stretch to suggest that without campaign donations, these acts may not have even been introduced, let alone become law. Had the acts not become law, the Financial Crisis and the Great Recession may never have occurred. *Campaign donations helped lead to the Financial Crisis and the Great Recession*, bringing our economy down and costing millions of people their homes, their jobs, and their livelihoods.

What it all Means

For those who wish to claim that campaign contributions do not matter much because they only influence "low visibility" legislation, the findings of this chapter hopefully serve as a wake-up call. Low profile notwithstanding, the GLBA of 1999 and the CFMA of 2000 legalized the activities that led to the Financial Crisis and the Great Recession—and campaign contributions were the single greatest factor leading to their passage.

As suggested in a report from the Center for Responsive Politics, banking donors wanted the GLBA (Ritsch 2008); they likely also wanted the CFMA. They gave money to lawmakers, and ultimately got what they wanted: the acts passed and their associated deregulations took effect. Within a decade, the economy came crashing down. Although the banks were certainly hit hard by the crash, they were also the beneficiaries of the government bailout. Those who suffered the most were ordinary citizens.

The Financial Crisis and ensuing Great Recession cost the economy upwards of $14trillion and had a terribly negative impact on ordinary folks. Nearly 8 million people lost their jobs during the recession; about 4 million people lost their homes *per year*. Unemployment skyrocketed during the recession, and the poverty rate soared to 15 percent. The Great Recession caused a lot of pain and suffering—yet it likely would not have happened if not for the influence of campaign contributions.

Campaign contributions clearly *do* matter. They provide donors with access to politicians; they also influence policy. As shown in this chapter, said influence comes at a hefty price: it can lead to financial crisis and bring down the economy. The Financial Crisis and ensuing Great Recession are good examples of this. In the next chapter, broader implications of campaign contributions for our economy will be examined—especially how they impact social inequality.

References

Baram, Marcus. 2008. "Who's Whining Now? Gramm Slammed by Economists." *ABC News*. https://abcnews.go.com/print?id=5835269

Burris, Val. 2005. "Interlocking Directorates and Political Cohesion among Corporate Elites." *American Journal of Sociology* 111, 249–283.

Institute for Policy Research. 2014. "The Great Recession: Over but Not Gone?" *Institute for Policy Research (IPR)*. www.ipr.northwestern.edu/about/news/2014/IPR-research-Great-Recession-unemployment-foreclosures-safety-net-fertility-public-opinion.html

Jones, Woodrow, Jr., and K. Robert Keiser. 1987. "Issue Visibility and the Effects of PAC Money." *Social Science Quarterly* 68:170–176.

Luttrell, David, Tyler Atkinson and Harvey Rosenblum. 2013. "Assessing the Costs and Consequences of the 2007–09 Financial Crisis and Its Aftermath." *DallasFed*, Economic Letter. www.dallasfed.org/~/media/Documents/research/eclett/2013/el1307.ashx

Mizruchi, Mark S. 1992. *The Structure of Corporate Political Action: Interfirm Relations and Their Consequences*. Cambridge, MA: Harvard University Press.

Riquier, Andrea. 2017. "Just One-Third of U.S. Homes have Recovered to Pre-Recession Levels." *MarketWatch*. www.marketwatch.com/story/only-one-third-of-american-home-values-have-recovered-pre-recession-peaks-2017-05-03

Ritsch, Massie. 2008. "Money and Votes Aligned in Congress's Last Debate Over Bank Regulation." *Open Secrets*. www.opensecrets.org/news/2008/09/money-and-votes-aligned-in-con/

Schram, Martin. 1995. *Speaking Freely: Former Members of Congress Talk about Money in Politics*. Washington, D.C.: Center for Responsive Politics.

5 Implications for Social Inequality

As shown in Chapter 4, campaign contributions can have a devastating effect on the economy. The Financial Crisis and subsequent Great Recession came about, in part, because donors lobbied for deregulation. The people who paid the price were ordinary citizens. Millions of people lost their jobs and their homes, and most Americans saw their financial wellbeing decline. Yet not everyone suffered equally during the Great Recession and its aftermath. In fact, the richest Americans actually saw their share of the nation's wealth *go up*. As asset values plummeted and the poverty rate rose to 15 percent, those at the top saw their assets recover in value very quickly, which increased their relative advantage (Fligstein and Rucks-Ahidiana 2016).

The disparities in how people fared during and after the Great Recession reflect a broader pattern in the US that has been ongoing since about 1980: the rich are getting richer and the poor are getting poorer. We are experiencing rising inequality. This is not without consequence: As inequality goes up, various problems emerge. Poverty rates rise, health issues expand, and life expectancy stagnates. Opportunities for upward mobility diminish, which keeps those at the bottom from moving up. It becomes a self-perpetuating cycle whereby the wealthy gain ever greater advantage while an increasing number of people find themselves in poverty, with few options to escape.

The political system contributes to inequality in multifaceted ways. Because the government sets policy related to regulations, contracts, subsidies, and the tax code, it can play a significant role in redistribution. But if the state has effectively been captured by the rich via campaign contributions, the government is unlikely to enact policy that would do much in the way of redistribution. This is where we are at today in the US. As I will elucidate in this chapter, things such as contract/subsidy disparities and the tax code largely

Implications for Social Inequality   53

favor the wealthy—likely because of campaign contributions and lobbying. But first, the recent history of inequality in the US will be described, followed by a discussion of why inequality matters.

Recent History of Inequality in the US

In the decades immediately following World War II, the US sported a robust middle class and had only moderate—if not low, by today's standards—levels of income inequality. This is when idyllic images of middle-class life—characterized by homeownership, the white picket fence, etc.—were popularized. Although there were certainly significant issues of gender and racial/ethnic inequality during this time period, it is nonetheless true that life was quite good for a sizeable proportion of the American citizenry. This began to change in the 1980s: the middle class began to shrink, and the groups at the ends of the distribution—the upper end—and, especially, the lower end—began to grow. In short, inequality began to rise in the 1980s, and has been rising steadily into the present.

Measuring Inequality

There are a number of different ways of measuring economic inequality. First, there is the matter of *what* one is going to focus on. Although there are numerous options, scholars typically focus on either income or wealth. Income is typically measured as money received in a particular timeframe (e.g. a year) from *all* sources, including one's job, investments, government assistance, etc. Importantly, scholars typically measure income *after* tax collection/disbursement given that taxes *can* be redistributive in nature. Income is a useful measure to use when thinking about economic inequality because income is directly tied with being able to afford the things one needs or desires in life—in other words, income is closely linked with standard of living. The higher one's income, the higher the person's standard of living; the lower one's income, the poorer the person's standard of living.

Wealth is usually measured as the net value of a person's assets. In other words, it is the market value of one's belongings—e.g. house, car, stocks, bonds, etc.—minus what the person owes on these items. As such, wealth can be a positive or a negative number. Wealth is a useful measure to use when thinking about income inequality because it gets at what is actually owned by segments of the population. There are a finite number of assets (e.g. property/land, stocks, etc.),

54 *Implications for Social Inequality*

so understanding who owns what share of these assets is illuminating. Moreover, wealth is related to income in important ways. For instance, some kinds of assets are income-producing, meaning that they produce a revenue stream for those who hold them. Examples include rental properties and dividend-paying stocks. Some wealthy individuals do not have jobs, per se, but are instead able to live off of income derived from their assets.

There are a few different ways of examining income and wealth disparities. One technique is to break the population into different segments—e.g. fifths, or "quintiles"—and compare the top with the bottom. For instance, the top quintile of earners in the US earn around 50 percent of the aggregate income; the bottom quintile earns just 5 percent of the income. With regards to wealth, the disparity is greater: the top quintile of wealth holders owns around 85 percent of the aggregate wealth; the bottom quintile actually has a net-negative wealth—they own around −1 percent of the wealth in the US. Examining quintiles can be illuminating, but it is a bit unhandy given that it relies on multiple numbers; a single number would be more straightforward. There is a measure that fits that description perfectly: the Gini coefficient.

The Gini coefficient—named after the Italian statistician who came up with the measure—is a single number that represents the percent of something that would have to be redistributed for that something to be equally distributed. So, in the case of income, the Gini coefficient is the percent of aggregate income that would have to be redistributed for income to be equally distributed. A Gini coefficient of zero would be perfect equality—everyone earns the same income; a Gini coefficient of 100 would be perfect *inequality*—one person earns *all* the income. For wealth, it is interpreted similarly: zero would mean that everyone has the same net assets; 100 would indicate that one person owns everything.

The Gini coefficient for income inequality is in the twenties or thirties in most developed countries. For instance, virtually all the countries in Western Europe are in the twenties or thirties; Australia and New Zealand are in the thirties; Japan is in the thirties; and our neighbor to the north, Canada, is in the low thirties. The US, however, is an exception to the rule: the Gini coefficient for income inequality in the US is around forty-eight. In other words, nearly half of the aggregate income in the US would have to be redistributed for income to be equally distributed. As described in the first paragraph of this section, inequality has risen since 1980—and the Gini coefficient for income inequality depicts this quite well. The Gini coefficient for income inequality in 1980 was around thirty-seven—on the high end for developed countries, but still within the "normal" range. By 1985, the Gini coefficient had risen to thirty-nine; by 1990, forty; in 1995, it was up to forty-two; by 2000, forty-three; in 2005, forty-five; by 2010, forty-seven; and in 2015 it reached a new high of forty-eight.

Although our Gini coefficient for income inequality of forty-eight is relatively high, our Gini coefficient for wealth inequality is much higher at eighty-seven (Keister 2005). In other words, 87 percent of our aggregate wealth would have to be redistributed for net assets to be distributed equally in the US. Knowing that the Gini coefficient's range is from zero to 100, this is getting awfully close to the scenario mentioned earlier in which one person owns *everything*. When we think about the net worth of some of our wealthiest individuals, this does not seem too far-fetched. Counting down the top three according to the most recent Forbes list, Warren Buffett is worth $84billion, Bill Gates is worth $90billion, and Jeff Bezos is worth a staggering $112billion—$112,000,000,000 (Kroll and Dolan 2018). To put things in perspective, these numbers are higher than many countries' entire annual economic output.

Why Inequality Matters

The fact that inequality is high and rising in the US should be of great concern to many people. Inequality, when it is too high, carries adverse consequences for society and the individuals within it, such as rising poverty, health issues, and a decrease in opportunities for upward mobility. I will discuss these consequences in this section; but first, it is worth describing the public's views of inequality.

Surveys of the American public consistently show that people underestimate how much inequality we have. For instance, when shown images of hypothetical distributions of income and asked which one best matches the income patterns in the US, people tend to select a picture that depicts a more equal distribution than what we actually have (Hauser and Norton 2017). Additionally, when asked about the disparity is between CEO pay and average worker compensation, they believe it is a 30:1 ratio (Kiatpongsan and Norton 2014) when in reality it is a whopping 373:1 ratio (AFL-CIO 2015). People are similarly uninformed about wealth inequality. As noted earlier, the top quintile of wealth holders owns around 85 percent of the aggregate net assets in the US. Yet when people are asked how much they think the top quintile owns, their answers average out to about 59 percent—more than 25 points lower than reality (Norton and Ariely 2011).

56 *Implications for Social Inequality*

As incorrect as people may be in their perceptions of the inequality structure, they strongly agree that it would be preferable to have less inequality. For example, in the study that asked about CEO pay versus average worker compensation, respondents felt that the ratio of CEO pay to worker pay *should* be just 7:1 (Kiatpongsan and Norton 2014)—a tiny fraction of the 373:1 ratio it is today (AFL-CIO 2015). In the study gauging perceptions of wealth inequality, people believed that the top quintile of wealth holders *should* own just 32 percent of the aggregate net assets—significantly less than the 85 percent they actually own (Norton and Ariely 2011).

Peoples' perceptions of inequality carry consequences. For instance, their feelings toward the justness of inequality can influence stress levels and relationship quality (Jasso 1999). People who feel that inequality is unjust are more likely to experience psychological distress—especially if they are on the low end of the stratification hierarchy (Mirowsky and Ross 2003). This, in turn, can lead to family strain and relationship issues. It can also lead to—or exacerbate—health issues. Psychological health and physical health are tightly linked.

Psychological distress is one important factor that can lead to health issues; poverty is another key variable. Inequality is often associated with poverty. With greater inequality, an increasing share of the resources is held by a decreasing percentage of people at the top while a growing proportion of the population sinks toward the bottom. Poverty rates are relatively high in the US, especially in comparison with other similarly developed nations. The overall poverty rate today is between 10 and 15 percent depending on the health of the economy (e.g. after the Great Recession, the poverty rate rose to 15 percent). More alarmingly, 20 percent of children in the US live in poverty. Poverty rates are much lower in European countries and the developed economies of Asia—likely because these countries have less inequality than we do.

Poverty can lead to serious issues. In extreme cases, poverty can lead to hunger and/or homelessness. But even outside of these extreme cases, it can lead to poor health. People in poverty are three times as likely as more affluent individuals to rate their health as just fair or poor. They also suffer from chronic conditions, such as diabetes and heart disease, at much higher rates than the population as a whole. More startlingly, people in poverty have lower life expectancies and are more likely to die prematurely than others.

Recent research published in the *Journal of the American Medical Association* (JAMA) shows that the rich live significantly longer than the poor in the US (Chetty et al. 2016). For instance, comparing the top 1 percent of income-earners with the bottom 1 percent, there is a nearly fifteen-year life expectancy gap among men and a ten-year gap among women: rich men live fifteen years longer than poor men, and rich women live ten years longer than poor women. Although this example looks at the tails of the distribution, there are differences at all levels of income: for instance, middle-income Americans live longer than low-income Americans, etc.

The relatively high levels of inequality and poverty in the US lead to poorer average health across the board—at least in comparison with other countries. Average life expectancies in the US are around seventy-nine (eighty-one for women, seventy-seven for men). This is lower than other developed nations, and places the US behind much of Europe, the developed countries of Asia, and even a few nations in the Americas such as Canada, Chile, and Costa Rica. Additionally, rising inequality means that progress in life expectancy will stagnate. This is exactly what is happening today in the US. Life expectancy in the US has actually declined slightly two years in a row—2016 and 2017 (Donnelly 2018). This is not supposed to happen in developed countries, but is happening here—likely because of our rising inequality.

Last but not least, inequality matters for mobility. We like to think of the US as a "land of opportunity." Rags-to-riches stories dating back to the work of Horatio Alger in the 1800s glorify the notion that with hard work and perseverance people can achieve upward mobility. Sadly, this is less true today than it was a few decades ago. Studies show that we have less upward mobility today than we did in the 1950s, 1960s, and 1970s. Moreover, upward mobility tends to occur in short steps rather than large leaps—for instance, from middle income to high income rather than from low to high (Blau and Duncan 1967).

The decline in mobility in the US is important for a number of reasons. First, it connects back to the notions of distributive justice mentioned at the beginning of this subsection. If people are not rewarded according to their work and effort, they will feel that the system is unjust, which can lead to all of the problems mentioned earlier (e.g. poverty, health issues, etc.). Second, it can slow innovation and growth in society. If people of great talent are unable to realize their potential, we all lose out—new discoveries are not made, new technologies are not developed, and new inventions are never created. It is in society's best interest for people of great talent to realize their potential and impact our world.

58 *Implications for Social Inequality*

Part of the reason for the decline in mobility in the US is the rise in inequality. With too much inequality, very few people are able to achieve upward mobility because resources and opportunities are largely held at the very top of the stratification hierarchy. To use a ladder as an analogy, as inequality becomes too great, the rungs on the ladder are too far apart for people to reach the next level. This is largely due to the advantages the rich have secured that help consolidate their wealth and make it more difficult for others to move up. How have they secured these advantages? Through contributions, lobbying, and influence on policy.

How Campaign Contributions Increase Inequality

As inequality has risen in the US and mobility has declined, *campaign contributions have risen at a steady rate.* For instance, when measured as a rate per person in the population, donations to presidential campaigns were just $0.71 per person in the US in 1980; by 2008, this had risen to $5.75 per person. Likewise, contributions to congressional campaigns were around $1.53 per person in 1982, but had risen to $5.95 per person by 2010. Granted, one must use some caution in interpreting correlations. After all, there are some things that happen to be correlated over time that are not, in fact connected—and correlation does not equal causation. But the fact that contributions and inequality have both been on the rise is probably no coincidence.

Campaign donors are typically among the most well-resourced individuals and entities in our society (Lessig 2011; Olsen-Phillips et al. 2015), and their contributions influence policy at a variety of stages (e.g. Hall and Wayman 1990; Peoples 2010), as already expounded in Chapter 3. As a result, the outcome of policy reflects elite interests rather than the public interest (Gilens and Page 2014). Government relations officers readily admit that their contributions and lobbying are not geared toward the public good. For instance, one person interviewed by Clawson et al. (1998) said, "We don't do things altruistically. We don't do things...because it's the right thing to do. There ought to be a bottom line approach to it" (p. 71).

There are a variety of ways in which campaign contributions could increase inequality. One of these ways was discussed in the book already: deregulation. Through deregulation, protections for ordinary citizens are wiped away to give special allowances to corporations. The results can be catastrophic, as illustrated in Chapter 3. Deregulation of the banking and finance industry led to the housing bubble, the Financial Crisis, and, ultimately, the Great Recession.

As important as deregulation is, it is only one way in which donations might increase inequality. In this chapter, three more will be explored: government contracts, subsidies, and the tax code.

Government Contracts

Government contracts can increase inequality in a number of ways. Perhaps the most obvious way is by creating inequality between firms. Companies that secure government contracts often wind up with stable sources of revenue for years due to their (ongoing) relationship with the government; businesses that do not secure contracts may not have the same stability in revenue streams. By extension, the workers at firms—and the communities within which they reside—can benefit greatly from government contracts. If contracts are awarded based on contributions or bribes, it raises significant questions about both the ethics of contract awards and the inequality that they can create. Sadly, this is exactly what happens in some cases.

Defense contracts were for sale to the highest bidder when Randall "Duke" Cunningham was involved. Cunningham was a member of Congress who sat on a key committee that oversaw the awarding of defense contracts. He proved very willing to exchange contracts for money, and even kept a price sheet indicating how much money he wanted for a contract of X size. For instance, he asked for $140,000 in exchange for a contract worth $16million, and sought $440,000 for a contract worth $25million. But outside of this egregious instance of bribery, is there evidence that contributions influence the awarding of contracts? Yes.

In a study of postwar contracts awarded by the US government following the wars in Iraq and Afghanistan, Hogan et al. (2006) find that contributions were a significant factor in determining which firms received contracts and which did not. Comparing the 135 companies that received contracts versus a randomly selected group of 135 renowned companies in the same sector(s), they find that "campaign donations, donation amounts, and corporate political connections in the form of lobbyists and political action committees are positively associated with the likelihood that a company will receive a post-war contract" (p. 284). In particular, they find that companies that employed the use of lobbyists and PACs were around four to five times as likely to receive a contract versus companies that did not employ these approaches.

The findings of Hogan et al. (2006) are important for a number of reasons. First, specific to the case they examined, it shows

60　Implications for Social Inequality

that the US's postwar expenditures in Iraq and Afghanistan were heavily tilted by campaign donations and related activities. Not only were the wars controversial, with many in the public growing to believe that we did not belong in them (Sussman 2007), the contracts themselves were met with public scrutiny. This is especially true of so-called "no-bid contracts" (contracts for which no "bids"—or estimates—were solicited)—some of which went to Vice President Dick Cheney's former company, Halliburton. This left many fuming about the appearance of favoritism.

Another reason why the findings of Hogan et al. (2006) are important is because they carry implications for how government contracts are awarded, more generally. If contracts are awarded because of "connections" (contributions, lobbying, etc.), it raises question about whether or not the best possible providers of those services are being selected. There is no compelling reason to believe that companies that employ lobbyists and PACs are any better suited to provide goods/services than companies that do not employ lobbyists and PACs. Contracts should go to the companies that are best at providing the products sought, not the best at "playing the game" and filling politicians' campaign coffers. In a related vein, the findings of Hogan et al. (2006) raise questions about the degree to which competition for government contracts is fair—if there is even competition at all.

Economists widely agree that competition is good for markets and consumers in that it ensures that the best services and products are offered at the most reasonable rates. This is why the government has enacted many antitrust laws over the years that help break down barriers to competition, such as monopolies. Yet awarding contracts based on contributions—and especially offering "no-bid" contracts—goes against these efforts and significantly reduces competition. If economists are correct, this means that consumers are getting a poorer quality outcome in the end. And given that the government, in theory, serves "the people"—and ordinary citizens are paying an increasing share of taxes relative to other entities (e.g. corporations)—the "consumers" in the case of government contracts are all of us as taxpayers.

Subsidies

As noted in Chapter 3, corporate lobbyists are likely to seek out subsidies for their clients, among other things (Godwin and Seldon 2002). According to research by Lopez (2003), PACs and associated lobbying firms have great success obtaining subsidies. In an examination of agriculture subsidies, Lopez finds that corporate PACs representing the farm industry do very well. He estimates that "$1 in contributions brings about $2,000 in policy transfers"—an incredible rate of return (p. 257).

Subsidies such as those examined by Lopez (2003) increase inequality in some of the same ways that government contracts do. If an industry—say, agriculture—receives subsidies while other industries do not, it can create inequality *between* industries. Put differently, some industries can rely on government assistance if they face difficult business cycles; other industries, however, may not have that same luxury. Likewise, much like with government contracts, subsidies targeted toward certain industries may decrease competition, which, again, is bad for markets and consumers.

Subsidies can create an additional form of inequality beyond what contracts can create: subsidies can divert money away from social programs and other initiatives that aid in public welfare. Unlike contracts, which effectively come out of earmarked funds that will go to *some* company regardless, subsidies come out of the budget and are offset through decreases in other budget areas. Lopez (2003) admits this in the case of agricultural subsidies: "Eliminating campaign contributions would significantly decrease agricultural subsidies, hurt farm groups, *benefit consumers and taxpayers, and increase social welfare by approximately $5.5 billion*" (p. 257, emphasis added here). In other words, the subsidies secured by PACs and lobbyists for the agricultural industry add up to approximately $5.5billion—money that could go toward social welfare or other programs. It is almost certain that the same could be said for subsidies that other industries rely on. Although farm subsidies are among the largest offered by the government, adding in other subsidies would certainly increase that sum. As such, subsidies clearly exacerbate inequality in our society— and campaign contributions play a significant role in this.

The Tax Code

The tax code can be used to drastically increase inequality. Taxes are monies collected by the government from various sources (e.g. corporate profits, individual income, etc.), which is then used to fund the government and its programs, pay its debt obligations, etc. As already noted, tax dollars that go toward government contracts or subsidies can sometimes result in inequality. But more generally, taxes affect inequality in the sense that they serve a redistributive function depending on (a) how much tax is collected from which sources and

62   *Implications for Social Inequality*

(b) how that tax money is used. Individuals, rather than corporations, are paying an increasing share of the taxes in the US—and individuals on the low end of the income distribution sometimes end up paying a higher percent than people with higher incomes. Additionally, it is becoming less and less true that the taxes collected help the poor, as important programs are being scaled down and cut.

With respect to individuals, although it is true that the US has a "progressive" tax system—meaning that those who earn more pay a higher percent of their income in taxes—much of this progression is at relatively low levels of income. For instance, for single individuals in 2017, the tax rate rapidly rises from 10 percent for those earning less than $9,325 per year to 25 percent for those earning $37,950. This rate of increase then slows down, and reaches the "peak" percentage of 39.6 percent when an earner reaches $418,400 in income. People making millions of dollars per year are taxed at that same maximum percentage of 39.6 percent—that is, if their income is from a job. Investment income is taxed at a much lower rate of 15 to 20 percent, depending on income. This led billionaire Warren Buffett (2011) to decry the current system, noting that he pays a lower percent on his taxes than people who earn money from jobs rather than from investments—including many people in his own office. As such, although high earners sometimes pay a higher percentage of their income in taxes, much of the increase in tax rates is at relatively *low* income levels (e.g. $9,375 to $37,950); and high earners who glean their income from investments actually pay a *lower* percentage of their income in taxes (15 to 20 percent) than many. Add in the fact that people can pass on up to $11million in assets ($22million for married couples) tax-free upon death, it is clear that wealthy individuals do not bear a significant proportion of the tax burden in the US. Their corporations, too, get off easy.

Corporations today are paying a decreasing share of the overall taxes in the US relative to individuals. According to data from the US Office of Management and Budget, overall tax receipts from corporations and individual taxpayers were roughly equal in the 1930s. For instance, in 1935, the government received $529million in taxes from corporations and $527million from individuals—a 1:1 ratio. This 1:1 ratio remained largely in place through the 1940s and 1950s. But by the 1960s, the amount corporations paid in taxes fell to about half what individuals paid. For instance, in 1965, corporations paid just $25billion in taxes while individuals paid $49billion—about a 1:2 ratio. By the 1970s, the ratio had widened to about 1:3, and by the 1980s the gap had stretched to 1:5. For instance, in 1985, receipts from corporations totaled $61billion, but receipts from individual payers added up to $335billion. The gap has remained large—around 1:5—since the 1980s. For instance, in the most recent year for which data are available—2017—corporations paid just under $300billion in taxes while individuals paid almost $1.6trillion—approximately a 1:5 ratio.

What the above means is that corporations are paying a smaller and smaller share of the overall taxes collected in the US while individual taxpayers are carrying a larger and larger load of the tax burden. When looking at the relative share of overall taxes paid via different sources (individuals, corporations, social security receipts, excise taxes, and "other" sources), corporations used to routinely account for 20 percent or more of the overall taxes paid. For instance, through much of the 1940s, 1950s, and 1960s, corporations accounted for anywhere from 20 to 40 percent of tax receipts in the US, depending on the year. Today, however, corporations typically account for 10 percent or less of total tax revenue. For example, corporations accounted for 9 percent of the taxes received in 2017. By contrast, individual taxpayers today pay nearly 50 percent of the overall taxes in the country. For instance, in 2017 individuals accounted for 48 percent of all tax receipts.

Granted, one could argue that during economic downturns, we would expect corporations to pay less given that they earn less. This was certainly true during the Great Recession. In 2009, at the height of the recession, corporate tax receipts fell to $138billion from $304billion just a year prior, and the percent of overall taxes contributed by corporations dropped from 12 percent in 2008 to less than 7 percent in 2009. That said, the general trend of declining corporate taxes as a share of total receipts has been occurring *independent* of ups and downs in the economy.

When looked at slightly differently—examining corporate taxes as a percentage of Gross Domestic Product (GDP)—we see a similar pattern: corporate taxes went from around 4 percent of GDP in the 1940s, 1950s, and 1960s to just 2 percent of GDP in the 1980s to the present (e.g. 1.5 percent of GDP in 2017). As such, no matter how one slices it, corporations pay a lesser share of taxes, relatively speaking, today than in the past. Do contributions have something to do with this pattern? According to corporate executives and PAC officers, they do.

In their interviews with corporate executives and PAC officers, Clawson et al. (1998) were surprised at the extent to which people cited tax changes and loopholes as their greatest accomplishments in the political realm. Clawson and colleagues estimate that around

90 percent of those they interviewed offered exactly that sort of example. And while they did not specifically ask about taxes, many people they interviewed went ahead and proudly touted examples of tax victories anyway: "this provision saved our company X million dollars" (p. 71). Clawson and colleagues attribute this to the fact that tax savings are quantifiable and related to a company's bottom line.

Unfortunately, this is very likely a zero-sum game. Despite claims that tax cuts on corporations and the wealthy will "trickle down" to the rest of society, trickle-down economics is a myth (Arndt 1983). The benefits of tax cuts on those at the top of the stratification hierarchy do not trickle down to the rest of society—those benefits stay at the top. In other words, what saves a corporation millions of dollars *costs* society that same amount in lost government revenue that could go toward social programs or infrastructure/development.

As noted above, individuals are paying a greater share of taxes today relative to the past to help compensate for the decline in tax receipts coming from corporations. Yet despite paying a greater share of the taxes, ordinary folks are not getting a greater share of government assistance. As tax revenues decline and budgets tighten, often the first programs targeted for cuts and/or elimination are the very policies that could help everyday people. In short, corporations and the wealthy get tax cuts and other benefits (e.g. corporate welfare in the form of subsidies and rebates to certain industries) at the expense of everyone else. The tax bill passed in 2017 is a perfect example of this.

In 2017 Congress passed the Tax Cuts and Jobs Act. Although claims were made suggesting that the bill will benefit all Americans, the reality is that most of the cuts go to corporations and the wealthy. It is the largest standalone tax cut on corporations in US history, bringing the base tax rate on corporations down to 21 percent from 35 percent (Long 2017). Estimates suggest that this will equate to a $1trillion tax cut on corporations over a decade (Long 2017), reducing their already low burden.

Individuals, too, will see a reduction from the Tax Cuts and Jobs Act—but not everyone will enjoy this cut equally. Although less affluent individuals will see a tax cut in the short term, those cuts disappear by 2026. Meanwhile, the wealthy will see significant, long-term benefits. For instance, the rich will pay a lower maximum rate—and the threshold to have to pay the maximum rate goes up under the new law. Additionally, the estate tax threshold increases as well, further benefitting the affluent. Before the new law, an individual could bequeath up to $5.5million ($11million for couples) tax-free; with the bill's passage, those numbers doubled to $11million for an individual and $22million for couples (Long 2017).

The Tax Cuts and Jobs Act is expected to result in $1.46trillion in lost tax revenue (Long 2017)—losses that will almost certainly be partially offset by cuts in social programs that help ordinary people. Right after the bill passed, (outgoing) Speaker of the House Paul Ryan began publicly discussing plans to cut welfare, Medicaid, and Medicare to reduce the deficit (Stein 2017)—a deficit *made worse by the tax bill*. In sum, the Tax Cuts and Jobs Act serves as a massive wealth transfer to corporations and the rich to the detriment of everyone else.

Although no one has done statistical analysis to determine the extent to which campaign contributions influenced the Tax Cuts and Jobs Act, there is certainly anecdotal evidence that donors wanted the bill (Blumenthal 2017). For instance, a number of nonprofits with ties to major donors ran ads in the days leading to the final vote, trying to persuade the public of the bill's merits—and pressure lawmakers to vote "yes" (Bykowicz 2017). The leader of a Super PAC with ties to Senate Majority Leader Mitch McConnell said with reference to the bill, "[Donors] would be mortified if we didn't live up to what we've committed to on tax reform" (Schultz 2017). Lawmakers implied—or even outright admitted—that their donors were effectively extorting them to pass the legislation. For instance, Senator Lindsey Graham was asked what would happen if the tax bill were to fail, and he replied, in part, that "[campaign] contributions would stop" (Thorp 2017). Representative Chris Collins was even more direct: "My donors are basically saying, 'Get it done or don't ever call me again'" (Marcos 2017).

Adding it all Up

Inequality has been on the rise in the US since around 1980. This has led to a decrease in opportunities for mobility as well as an increase in poverty. It has also contributed to health issues, as our overall life expectancy in the US is stagnating. The government could do something about our rising inequality, but it doesn't. In fact, it has contributed to the problem. Much of the reason why is because politicians act in the interest of their donors and elites rather than the public (Gilens and Page 2014). In short, campaign contributions help ensure that inequality is high and rising in the US.

Three specific ways in which contributions increase inequality are through their impact on contracts, subsidies, and the tax code.

66 *Implications for Social Inequality*

Government contracts, if awarded unfairly (e.g. based on campaign donations), can create inequality between firms and can result in poorer quality goods/services. Subsidies create inequality between industries and may lead to offsetting cuts in other areas. The tax code can greatly increase inequality through cutting taxes on the wealthy and/or corporations and increasing the tax burden on ordinary individuals; lawmakers can exacerbate this inequality by cutting programs for the poor as a way of offsetting reductions in revenue from the wealthy/corporations.

This chapter discussed the above patterns in general terms and provided examples of each type of relationship. For instance, with respect to government contracts, the example of postwar contracts in Iraq and Afghanistan was highlighted, as Hogan et al. (2006) find that contributions were a significant factor in the awarding of such postwar contracts. In terms of the tax code, the example of Tax Cuts and Jobs Act of 2017 was raised. Anecdotal evidence suggests that donors pushed strongly for the act, and even threatened to cease giving contributions if lawmakers did not vote for it.

Policymakers make decisions that reflect the interests of elites rather than the interests of the general public (Gilens and Page 2014), and these decisions greatly impact the distribution of income and wealth in our country. Through their decisions on government contracts and the tax code, policymakers can tilt the system in favor of the wealthy. As illustrated in this chapter, campaign contributions influence this process. As a result, donations contribute to our increasing inequality in society. They also contribute to the undermining of our very democracy.

References

AFL-CIO. 2015. "Executive Paywatch: High-Paid CEOs and the Low-Wage Economy." www.aflcio.org/Corporate-Watch/Paywatch-2015

Arndt, H. W. 1983. "The 'Trickle-Down' Myth." *Economic Development and Cultural Change* 32(1):1–10.

Blau, Peter M. and Otis D. Duncan. 1967. *The American Occupational Structure*. New York: Wiley & Sons.

Blumenthal, Paul. 2017. "Republicans Admit that CEOs and Donors Really Need the Tax Cut Bill to Pass—or Else." *Huffington Post*. www.huffington post.com/entry/gary-cohn-tax-cut-ceos-donors_us_5a049571e4b0f76b 05c4249e

Buffett, Warren. 2011. "Stop Coddling the Super-Rich." *New York Times*. www.nytimes.com/2011/08/15/opinion/stop-coddling-the-super-rich.html

Bykowicz, Julie. 2017 "Groups Spend Tens of Millions to Sell Tax Bill to Middle Class: Advertising Push from GOP-Aligned Organizations Comes as Many Americans Remain Undecided on Overhaul." *Wall Street Journal*. www.wsj.com/articles/groups-spend-tens-of-millions-to-sell-tax-bill-to-middle-class-1510240495

Chetty, Raj, Michael Stepner, Sarah Abraham, Shelby Lin, Benjamin Scuderi, Nicholas Turner, Augustin Bergeron, and David Cutler. 2016. "The Association between Income and Life Expectancy in the United States, 2001–2014." *JAMA* 315(16):1750–1766. https://doi.org/10.1001/jama.2016.4226

Clawson, Dan, Alan Neustadtl, and Mark Weller. 1998. *Dollars and Votes: How Business Campaign Contributions Subvert Democracy*. Philadelphia: Temple University Press.

Donnelly, Grace. 2018. "Here's Why Life Expectancy in the U.S. Dropped again this Year." *Fortune*. http://fortune.com/2018/02/09/us-life-expectancy-dropped-again/

Fligstein, Neil and Zawadi Rucks-Ahidiana. 2016. "The Rich Got Richer: The Effects of the Financial Crisis on Household Well-Being, 2007–2009." Pp. 155–185 in *A Gedenkschrift to Randy Hodson: Working with Dignity (Research in the Sociology of Work, Volume 28)*, edited by Lisa A. Keister and Vincent J. Roscigno. Bingley, UK: Emerald.

Gilens, Martin, and Benjamin I. Page. 2014. "Testing Theories of American Politics: Elites, Interest Groups, and Average Citizens." *Perspectives on Politics* 12: 564–581.

Godwin, R. Kenneth, and Barry J. Seldon. 2002. "What Corporations Really Want from Government: The Public Provision of Private Goods." Pp. 205–224 in *Interest Group Politics*, 6th Ed., edited by Allan J. Cigler and Burdett A. Loomis. Washington, D.C.: Congressional Quarterly Press.

Hall, Richard L., and Frank W. Wayman. 1990. "Buying Time: Moneyed Interests and the Mobilization of Bias in Congressional Committees." *American Political Science Review* 84:797–820.

Hauser, Oliver P. and Michael I. Norton. 2017. "(Mis)perceptions of Inequality." *Current Opinion in Psychology* 18:21–25.

Hogan, Michael J., Michael A. Long, and Paul B. Stretesky. 2006. "Campaign Contributions, Post-War Reconstruction Contracts, and State Crime." *Deviant Behavior* 27:269–297.

Jasso, Guillermina. 1999. "How Much Injustice Is There in the World? Two New Justice Indexes." *American Sociological Review* 64:133–168.

Keister, Lisa A. 2005. *Getting Rich: America's New Rich and How They Got That Way*. New York: Cambridge University Press.

Kiatpongsan, Sorapop and Michael I. Norton. 2014. "How Much (More) Should CEOs Make? A Universal Desire for More Equal Pay." *Perspectives on Psychological Science* 9:587–593. https://doi.org/10.1177/1745691614549773

Kroll, Luisa and Kerry Dolan (Eds.). 2018. "Meet The Members of the Three-Comma Club." *Forbes*. www.forbes.com/billionaires/#7976a14d251c

68 Implications for Social Inequality

Lessig, Lawrence. 2011. *Republic, Lost: How Money Corrupts Congress—and a Plan to Stop It.* New York: Twelve.

Long, Heather. 2017. "The Final GOP Tax Bill Is Complete: Here's What Is In It." *Washington Post.* www.washingtonpost.com/news/wonk/wp/2017/12/15/the-final-gop-tax-bill-is-complete-heres-what-is-in-it/

Lopez, Rigoberto A. 2003. "Campaign Contributions and Agricultural Subsidies." *Economics and Politics* 13:257–279. https://doi.org/10.1111/1468-0343.00093

Marcos, Cristina. 2017. "GOP Lawmaker: Donors Are Pushing Me to Get Tax Reform Done." *The Hill.* http://thehill.com/homenews/house/359110-gop-lawmaker-donors-are-pushing-me-to-get-tax-reform-done

Mirowsky, John, and Catherine E. Ross. 2003. *Social Causes of Psychological Distress,* 2nd Ed. New York: Aldine.

Norton, Michael I. and Dan Ariely. 2011. "Building a Better America—One Wealth Quintile at a Time." *Perspectives on Psychological Science* 6: 9–12. https://doi.org/10.1177/1745691610393524

Olsen-Phillips, Peter, Russ Choma, Sarah Bryner and Doug Weber. 2015. "The Political One Percent of the One Percent in 2014: Mega Donors Fuel Rising Cost of Elections." *OpenSecrets News. Center for Responsive Politics.* www.opensecrets.org/news/2015/04/the-political-one-percent-of-the-one-percent-in-2014-mega-donors-fuel-rising-cost-of-elections/

Peoples, Clayton D. 2010. "Contributor Influence in Congress: Social Ties and PAC Effects on U.S. House Policymaking." *The Sociological Quarterly* 51:649–677.

Schultz, Marisa. 2017. "GOP's Big Donors Threaten to Close Wallets if Tax Reform Isn't Passed." *New York Post.* https://nypost.com/2017/11/06/gops-big-donors-threaten-to-close-wallets-if-tax-reform-isnt-passed/

Stein, Jeff. 2017. "Ryan Says Republicans to Target Welfare, Medicare, Medicaid Spending in 2018." *Washington Post.* www.washingtonpost.com/news/wonk/wp/2017/12/01/gop-eyes-post-tax-cut-changes-to-welfare-medicare-and-social-security/?utm_term=.be53b6efee57

Sussman, Dalia. 2007. "Poll Shows View of Iraq War Is Most Negative Since Start." *New York Times.* www.nytimes.com/2007/05/25/washington/25view.html

Thorp, Frank. 2017. *Twitter.* https://twitter.com/frankthorp/status/928649996311900160?ref_src=twsrc%5Etfw&ref_url=http%3A%2F%2Fthehill.com%2Fpolicy%2Ffinance%2F359606-graham-financial-contributions-will-stop-if-gop-doesnt-pass-tax-reform

6 Implications for our Democracy

Democracy versus Autocracy, Oligarchy

Democracy can be defined in a number of different ways. At its core, though, democracy refers to rule by the people. Autocracy, on the other hand, refers to rule by a small handful of people—or a single dictator. Democracy and autocracy exist on opposite ends of a political spectrum. Democracy, on the one end, is a situation in which the "people"—ordinary citizens—have a strong voice in the system. Autocracy, on the other end, is a situation in which a small group of leaders make decisions and ordinary people have little say in political decisions. Some characteristics of democracy include free and fair elections, freedom of speech, and easy access to one's political representatives. Some features of autocracies are sham elections, if any; repression of speech/rights; and virtually no access to political leaders except through money/bribes.

Although the US generally scores high on indexes of democratization, it is by no means the most democratic country in the world. Indeed, I will argue in this chapter that we are further from the ideal conception of democracy than many would like to admit—and much of the reason why has to do with our campaign finance system. Because of our campaign finance system, we have become an example of a *third* kind of system called "oligarchy" (also known as plutocracy)—a system in which only the wealthy have their voices heard (in other words, rule of "the few" or "the rich").

In the following paragraphs and pages, I will begin by discussing each of the features and characteristics one would expect in a healthy democracy—and I will demonstrate the ways in which we fall short of these ideals. I will then explain how our campaign finance system promotes bribery, organizational deviance, institutional corruption, and state-corporate crime. I will conclude by discussing the implications of all of this for our political system—and how it illustrates that we have an oligarchy in the US.

70 *Implications for our Democracy*

Free and Fair Elections

In theory, the US has free and fair elections. But there are a number of problems with our elections that cannot go ignored. One of the problems is our Electoral College system. In presidential elections, we do not have direct elections characterized by one person, one vote. Instead, how we elect our president is through assigning a certain number of points, or electors, per state, then awarding those points to the winner of that state. For most states, it is a "winner takes all" scenario in which the candidate who gets the majority of votes—even if it is a slim majority (e.g. 50.1 percent)—is awarded all of the state's electors. Only Nebraska and Maine award their points proportionally.

Under the "point" system of the Electoral College, it is possible for the candidate winning the popular vote to end up with fewer points than their opponent, and, thus, lose the election. In fact, it has happened twice since 2000. In the 2000 election, Al Gore received the majority of the popular vote, but failed to win as many Electoral College points as George W. Bush. As such, George W. Bush was elected president despite losing the popular vote. In 2016, we saw a similar scenario: Hillary Clinton won the popular vote by nearly 3 million votes, but she did not receive as many Electoral College points as her opponent, Donald Trump. As a result, Donald Trump was elected president.

In addition to our problematic Electoral College system, we have other challenges connected to our elections. For instance, not everyone who should have the right to vote is actually given that privilege. Many states have strict voter ID laws that require people to present a valid photo ID to vote. Often the rationale behind such laws is to prevent voter fraud (e.g. voting for someone else, voting multiple times)—but there is very little evidence of voter fraud. For instance, in the 2016 election, there were only four documented cases of voter fraud (Bump 2016). The problem with voter ID laws is that not everyone has a photo ID. Moreover, those individuals least likely to have a valid photo ID are often the most disenfranchised in our society—the poor and racial/ethnic minorities. As such, those in the most desperate of economic circumstances in our society are often the very individuals who are denied the opportunity to vote and have a voice. Unfortunately, an increasing number of states are moving in the direction of enacting voter ID laws, which will only further voter disenfranchisement.

Another problem with elections in the US is gerrymandering. Gerrymandering is the process through which district lines are redrawn in ways that virtually guarantee electoral success for one party or another. The result is districts that look less like sensible shapes and look more like sea monsters—grotesque and contorted with tentacles reaching here and there. Many districts are not very competitive as it is. Some districts are reliably democratic; other districts are reliably republican. Although not a universal pattern, urban districts tend to be democratic whereas rural districts tend to be republican. But gerrymandering has exacerbated this pattern and led some districts to be, effectively, "always democratic" or "always republican." This pattern helps contribute to the fact that many elections themselves are tilted.

Are elections in the US "free and fair?" Based on the evidence presented in Chapter 3, US elections are neither free nor fair. It costs a lot of money to run a successful campaign. The sorts of things that help one win office—canvassing, advertising, etc.—all cost money. As such, elections are far from free, at least in the monetary sense. Additionally, the candidate that spends the most typically wins. Consequently, elections are not fair. Candidates that do not have access to troves of campaign cash have a far lower likelihood of being elected—independent of their stance on issues or their willingness to work on behalf of their constituents. In fact, such candidates are unlikely to even reach the general election stage—they will be weeded out in the "money primary." Our campaign finance system clearly contributes to problems with our elections.

Freedom of Speech

The First Amendment protects free speech in the US. Under the First Amendment, people are allowed to express their views without fear of state repression. The First Amendment provides freedom of assembly, freedom of the press (media), etc. It is certainly true that individuals in the US have more freedom to express themselves than people in some other nations. In countries governed by strict authoritarian regimes, speaking negatively about political leadership could result in imprisonment or death—for instance, reports people are routinely imprisoned or killed in North Korea if they do not express enthusiastic support for the "Supreme Leader." In some other countries, forming a social movement may result in the same fate—imprisonment or death. A good example of this is the Chinese government's response to pro-democracy demonstrations in 1989. The government sent troops and tanks into Tiananmen Square in Beijing to squash the movement. Although no one is sure, estimates

72 *Implications for our Democracy*

suggest that more than 1,000 protesters were imprisoned or executed in the aftermath of the demonstrations.

As above, individual citizens have freedom to express themselves in the US without fear of reprisal. But who is listening? It makes little difference to have freedom of expression if one's views are falling on deaf ears or are being ignored by policymakers. Unfortunately, this is exactly what is happening in the US today. Although people have some voice via social movements, individuals have little voice with policymakers.

As noted in Chapter 3, policymakers pay attention to donors and their lobbyists. Evidence suggests that they pay far less attention to ordinary constituents—and policy decisions reflect this bias (Gilens and Page 2014). It appears, then, that in the US, "free speech" is anything but free. To have an audible voice in the system, one needs to pay a sum in the form of campaign contributions. Without paying this price, speech will likely be ignored. This has strong connections with access—or lack thereof—to policymakers.

Access to Leaders

As noted in Chapter 3, one of the benefits of campaign contributions for donors is access to policymakers. While some donors deny that contributions result in policy outcomes, few deny that contributions provide access (Schram 1995). If one has given a campaign contribution to a politician, phone calls will be answered, appointments will be granted. If one has not donated money, getting a response from a policymaker—or especially meeting with them—is highly unlikely. At the state/local levels, getting a response or meeting is more likely (though not guaranteed); at the federal level, one might as well forget it. The response one receives will most likely be from a staff member; actually meeting with someone may be virtually impossible. As noted earlier, former member of Congress Mick Mulvaney summarized it quite well: "If you're a lobbyist who never gave us money, I didn't talk to you. If you're a lobbyist who gave us money, I might talk to you" (Thrush 2018).

If policymakers are not responsive to those who request their time, but, instead, effectively require monetary contributions for access, it is again true that there is little "free" about our political system. More importantly, our system is beginning to look similar to the authoritarian regimes of the world, where violations, bribery, and corruption prevail. Sadly, these are prominent features of the system in the US.

Violations of the Law

There have been numerous infractions over the years related to our campaign finance system. A very recent example involves a former attorney of Donald Trump, Michael Cohen, who pleaded guilty in August of 2018 to eight criminal counts—including two violations of campaign finance law—and was ultimately sentenced to three years in prison for his crimes (Weiser and Rashbaum 2018). In the first count of breaking campaign finance rules, Cohen admitted to causing a corporation to give a campaign contribution (illegal dating back to the FECA regulations discussed in Chapter 2). In the second count, Cohen admitted to giving individual contributions to a candidate in excess of the current limits. Both counts, in their entirety, are provided below, verbatim from the US Attorney's (2018) charges filed in the Southern District of New York.

Count 1 ("Count 7" in the full document): Causing an Unlawful Corporate Contribution

From in or about June 2016, up to and including in or about October 2016, in the Southern District of New York and elsewhere, MICHAEL COHEN, the defendant, knowingly and willfully caused a corporation to make a contribution and expenditure, aggregating $25,000 and more during the 2016 calendar year, to the campaign of a candidate for President of the United States, to wit, COHEN caused Corporation-1 to make and advance a $150, 000 payment to Woman-1, including through the promise of reimbursement, so as to ensure that Woman-1 did not publicize damaging allegations before the 2016 presidential election and thereby influence that election.

Count 2 ("Count 8" in the full document): Excessive Campaign Contribution

On or about October 27, 2016, in the Southern District of New York and elsewhere, MICHAEL COHEN, the defendant, knowingly and willfully made and caused to be made a contribution to Individual-1, a candidate for Federal office, and his authorized political committee in excess of the limits of the Election Act, which aggregated $25,000 and more in calendar year 2016, and did so by making and causing to be made an expenditure, in cooperation, consultation, and concert with, and at the request

74 *Implications for our Democracy*

and suggestion of one or more members of the campaign, to wit, COHEN made a $130,000 payment to Woman-2 to ensure that she did not publicize damaging allegations before the 2016 presidential election and thereby influence that election.

Although both counts in the Cohen case involve contributions that were not explicitly provided as campaign donations, they were nonetheless tantamount to campaign contributions in that they were given, in part, to influence the election by helping cover up alleged affairs that, if publicized, would have been damaging to a candidate in the presidential race. One especially important element in this case is that when Cohen pleaded guilty, he told the judge that he was directed to orchestrate the illegal campaign contributions by "a candidate." This implicates said candidate in federal crimes and has led some to speculate that it could possibly lead to impeachment proceedings (Helderman et al. 2018).

Bribery

A number of high-profile bribery cases involving politicians have splashed the headlines over the past couple of decades. One of the more famous cases involved the now-infamous lobbyist Jack Abramoff. Abramoff pleaded guilty to conspiracy/corruption, among other things. In the press release announcing Abramoff's guilty plea, the US Department of Justice (2006) wrote the following:

Abramoff…admitted that as one means of accomplishing results for their clients, he [and others] engaged in a pattern of corruptly providing things of value to public officials…with the intent to influence acts by the public officials that would benefit Abramoff and Abramoff's clients. For example, [Abramoff and others] provided things of value to a public official [described as Representative #1] and members of his staff, including, but not limited to, a lavish trip to Scotland to play golf on world-famous courses… and campaign contributions for the Representative, his political action committee, his campaign committee, and other political committees on behalf of the Representative. At the same time, and in exchange for these things of value, [Abramoff and others] sought and received the Representative's agreement to perform directly and through others a series of official acts, including but not limited to agreements to support and pass legislation, and agreements to place statements in the Congressional Record.

Implications for our Democracy   75

It was later revealed that "Representative #1" in the Department of Justice press release was Bob Ney, a House member from Ohio. As the press release indicates, Ney received generous campaign contributions from Abramoff and was provided with a lavish vacation to Scotland. In return, Ney offered help on legislation of interest to Abramoff. Ney ultimately pleaded guilty to false statements and conspiracy. He spent seventeen months in prison for his crimes (Nash 2008).

James Traficant, another House member from Ohio, was charged with bribery, racketeering, filing false tax returns, and other crimes in the early 2000s (CNN 2002). He represented himself in court, which he had done about twenty years prior when he was charged with—but acquitted of—bribery when serving as a County Sheriff. But this time, he was not acquitted; instead, he was found guilty on all counts and ultimately served a seven-year prison sentence.

A rather famous case of bribery involved a member of the House from California, Randall "Duke" Cunningham. Cunningham headed a committee that decided on defense contracts. In his role, it appears he effectively sold defense contracts to the highest bidders. He kept a "price sheet" that listed the amounts of money he wanted for a contract of X size (e.g. $140,000 for a $16million contract). (See Figure 6.1 for a picture and description of Duke Cunningham's price sheet he kept concerning contracts.) A defense contractor purchased Cunningham's home for $700,000 above its eventual sale

Figure 6.1 "Duke" Cunningham's list of bribe amounts he requested from clients in exchange for respective government contracts (contract amounts are on the left, in millions; bribe amounts are on the right, starting at $140,000 and going up in $50,000 or $25,000 increments). (Image source: US Department of Justice)

76 *Implications for our Democracy*

price (Stern 2005). That same contractor allowed Cunningham to stay in a yacht rent-free while he was in Washington D.C.—a yacht named "Duke Stir" (Bennett 2005). All told, he accepted upwards of $2.4million in bribes, and he served seven years in prison for his crimes (Condon 2014).

Perhaps the most unusual case in recent years involved William Jefferson, a member of the US House from Louisiana. He was sentenced to thirteen years in prison, of which he served approximately five before being released after a judge threw out seven of the ten charges against him. But what makes the case unusual is where the FBI found some of the evidence they used in the case against him: when they did a search, they found around $90,000 hidden *in his freezer* (Lengel 2006). Certainly gives new meaning to the expression "cold, hard cash!"

Are Contributions Bribery?

Although the above cases make for interesting reading and represent egregious cases of bribery, an important question emerges when examining such scandals: Are contributions tantamount to bribes? Former Senator Russell Long once famously said that "the distinction between a campaign contribution and a bribe is almost a hairline's difference" (Kaiser 2009:18). They are not, however, typically considered bribes—at least not in a legal sense.

The reason why contributions are not considered bribes in a legal sense has to do with the juxtaposition of the *Federal Bribery Statute* and the way in which current campaign finance laws are written (Chapter 8 will discuss the conflict of interest in the fact that policymakers get to write their own rules—including campaign finance regulations). It is also related to *how* the exchanges typically occur.

According to the *Federal Bribery Statute* (18 *U.S. Code* 201), it is illegal for any public official to receive or accept "anything of value… in return for being influenced in the performance of any official act." Contributions are clearly "of value" to lawmakers as they seek election and reelection. Yet the campaign finance laws outlined in Chapter 2 allow campaign contributions to be freely given/received, meaning that donations are technically legal. This has been supported in the courts.

In the 1991 *McCormick v. United States*, 500 U.S. 257, Supreme Court decision, Justice Anthony Kennedy argued that "to hold that legislators commit federal crime when they act for the benefit of constituents shortly before or after campaign contributions are solicited and received...is an unrealistic assessment...but [it could be a crime] if the payments are made in return for an *explicit promise* or undertaking by the official to perform or not to perform an official act" (emphasis added here). This suggests that even being influenced by contributions may not, in fact, count as bribery in the eyes of the law. Only quid pro quo exchanges would count as bribery.

A quid pro quo exchange is one in which a promise is made in exchange for payment. What this means for lawmakers is that, for instance, promising to vote "yea" on a bill in exchange for a campaign contribution would be a case of bribery; happening to vote "yea" on a bill after a contributor made a compelling case for voting that way would *not* be bribery. In the first instance, a promise has been made, making it a quid pro quo exchange; in the second instance, no promise has been made. The outcome is the same in both instances, but the first is against the law while the second is technically legal.

Although the above discussion clarifies that contributions—and even being influenced by contributions—is technically legal under our present system, it does not mean that they meet societal norms/expectations regarding behavior. By societal standards, contributions can still be viewed as akin to bribes—and their influence seen as a form of deviance.

Organizational Deviance

Deviance refers to anything that falls outside societal norms/expectations. Some forms of deviance are outlawed and have formal sanctions in place against them, which means they are also criminal. Other deviant acts, however, are not formally outlawed, and, thus, may not be criminal—but are deviant nonetheless.

It is important to note that deviant acts can be performed by both individuals and larger entities/organizations (Ermann and Lundman 1978). Referred to as "organizational deviance," such deviant acts must meet four conditions: (1) they must go against external norms, (2) they must find support within the organization, (3) they must be known by those at the top, and (4) new members must be socialized into those same acts.

Violating External Norms

One can certainly make the case that contributions and their influence go against external norms. As seen in the opinion polls cited in Chapter 1, the general public is opposed to our current campaign

78   *Implications for our Democracy*

finance system and wants reform (Mayer 2001). Contributions are therefore contrary to societal norms. But contributions may even go against political norms. Outside of elected positions, political actors cannot accept contributions. It is only for elected positions that those seeking political posts can solicit and accept campaign contributions.

Support within Politics

Contributions are clearly supported within political bodies. Virtually all congressional candidates—except for those who are independently wealthy—accept campaign contributions. Indeed, they spend a lot of time soliciting donations—more than 50 percent of their time, by some estimates (Lessig 2011). Presidential candidates can sign on to a system of partial public funding, but all but one of the dozens of recent presidential candidates have opted out of the partial public funding option—and *all* of the candidates have accepted campaign contributions from private donors.

There is mounting evidence that being influenced by contributors is widely supported practice in political bodies. My own work, which, again, models contributor influence in social network terms, shows a statistically significant general influence of contributions on voting in the US House (Peoples 2010). This would not be the case if these were simply the actions of a "few bad apples" (Peoples and Sutton 2015), as the actions of those few individuals would not be enough to create a statistically significant effect. As a result, it is safe to assume that being influenced by donors is common practice that is condoned by political actors.

Known at the Top

Contributions—and their influence—are supported at the highest levels of American politics. As noted above, all presidential candidates have accepted private donations to their campaigns, signaling to candidates at other levels that this is accepted practice. Moreover, House and Senate leaders not only receive contributions, but often establish their own "leadership PACs" as noted in Chapter 4, which allow them to solicit money from donors, pool it, and then donate it to other members of Congress to help their campaigns and potentially earn their allegiance. Indeed, there is a strong correlation between being in leadership positions and having large leadership PACs. As such, donating campaign cash is a practice that is not only known at the top, but is condoned and practiced by congressional leaders.

Socializing New Members

New lawmakers are socialized into the culture of campaign contributions. They are sometimes invited to fundraisers by more senior politicians as a way of introducing them to donors—and socializing them into a culture of contributions. It apparently rubs off quickly: as noted earlier, freshmen lawmakers are influenced by contributions, just as their more senior colleagues are (Peoples 2010). There is a culture in American politics around contributions, exchange of favors, etc., and even those individuals at the very earliest stages of their careers very quickly learn the ropes and engage in the process.

Based on the above, it seems clear that contributor influence on American politics could be viewed as organizational deviance, particularly in the case of a body such as Congress (Peoples and Sutton 2015). These actions meet all four conditions introduced by Ermann and Lundman (1978) and outlined above. This implies that our political system may also meet the definition of a new term among ethics scholars: institutional corruption.

Institutional Corruption

The Edmond J. Safra Center for Ethics at Harvard University established a research lab to study, among other things, what the Center referred to as "institutional corruption." Although the definition of the term was a working definition that changed over time, the generally agreed upon definition is as follows:

> Institutional corruption is manifest when there is a systemic and strategic *influence* which is *legal*, or even currently ethical, that *undermines the institution's effectiveness* by diverting it from its purpose or weakening its ability to achieve its purpose, including, to the extent relevant to its purpose, *weakening* either *the public's trust* in that institution or the institution's inherent trustworthiness.
>
> (Lessig 2013; emphasis added here)

I was affiliated with the Edmond J. Safra Center for Ethics for two years as a fellow. While serving as a fellow, I made the case with others that campaign contributions were causing institutional corruption in Congress and other political bodies. The reasoning behind the argument follows the logic of the definition presented above.

First and foremost, campaign contributions do have a systematic and strategic influence. As established in previous chapters, contributions

80 *Implications for our Democracy*

influence elections and policy, and contributors give money in a strategic fashion to enhance their influence.

As highlighted in the definition, institutional corruption need not be illegal. This is certainly true of campaign contributions. As the discussion earlier in the chapter highlighted, contributions are legally allowed in our current campaign finance system.

Campaign contributions divert our political institutions from their intended purpose—serving the people—which ultimately undermines the institutions' effectiveness. Lessig (2011) makes the case that while our political bodies ought to be dependent upon the people alone—indeed, this was the guiding principle of our Republic instilled by the founding fathers—campaign contributions create a "competing dependency." In other words, politicians have become dependent upon contributions to increase their odds of (re)election, and therefore have two distinct, sometimes opposing constituencies: their contributors and the people. Research suggests that contributors end up with far greater say in policy than the people (Gilens and Page 2014).

Campaign contributions have likely contributed to the crisis of trust that we now see with Congress and other political bodies. As already noted, the public believes that Congress is corrupt and that Congress favors special interests over constituent concerns (e.g. Dugan 2015). Moreover, polls show a very low approval rating for Congress. In fact, recent polls have shown Congress's approval to typically fall below 20 percent, and below 10 percent at times—a low figure, indeed (Gallup 2019). A recent poll even found that Congress was less popular than traffic jams, root canals, and cockroaches (Public Policy Polling 2013). One of the few things *less* popular than Congress, according to that same poll: lobbyists.

Given all of the above, it is clear that our campaign finance system in the US effectively creates institutional corruption. Campaign contributions influence policy decisions (e.g. Peoples 2010), and these decisions reflect elite interests rather than the public interest (Gilens and Page 2014). This culture of influence decreases the trust people have in our institutions such as Congress. All combined, it is clear that campaign contributions lead to institutional corruption. They may also lead to crime.

State–Corporate Crime

There is a growing literature in criminology and criminal justice around state crime and state-corporate crime. Chambliss (1989) defines state crime as "acts defined by law as criminal and committed by state officials in the pursuit of their job as representatives of the state" (p. 184). But Ross (2015) contends that state crime can also include things that are more generally "deviant, abusive, harmful [or] wrongful" (p. 499)—in other words, not only actions that are defined by law as criminal. This is an important addition to the definition of state crime, because state actors are in the unique position of being able to make, interpret, or enforce laws; accordingly, they have a say in what is deemed criminal and what is not. The scholarly definition of state crime should therefore not be restricted to only those acts defined by law as criminal.

In a similar vein, state-corporate crime should be defined broadly. The most generally accepted definition suggests that state-corporate crime involves "illegal or socially injurious actions that result from a mutually reinforcing interaction between (1) policies and/or practices in pursuit of the goals of one or more institutions of political governance and (2) policies and/or practices in pursuit of the goals of one or more institutions of economic production and distribution" (Aulette and Michalowski 1993:175). Note that much like ideal definitions of state crime, this definition is not contingent upon something being defined by law as criminal. For instance, "socially injurious actions" need not be criminal in a legal sense—they are simply actions that cause harm to others.

As demonstrated in Chapters 4 and 5, contributor influence can sometimes be socially injurious. Take, for instance, the influence that led to the passage of the Gramm-Leach-Bliley Act (GLBA) in 1999 and the Commodity Futures Modernization Act (CMFA) in 2000. These two bills led to the inflation—and ultimate popping—of the housing bubble in the US. This, in turn, led to the housing crisis and resultant Great Recession. Total losses added up to trillions of dollars, and millions of people lost their homes and/or their jobs. The fact that contributions helped sway lawmakers toward the passage of these Acts demonstrates that contributor influence can, indeed, be harmful to society. Consequently, we can say that campaign contributions can sometimes result in state-corporate crime. As a coauthor and I argued, "the outcome of any instance of contributor influence could potentially represent a unique case study in state-corporate crime" (Peoples and Sutton 2015:122).

Main Takeaways

The preceding paragraphs and pages have discussed various dimensions of our political system—and explored how campaign contributions connect to these dimensions. First, the definition of democracy

82 *Implications for our Democracy*

was presented and broken down into key elements, such as free and fair elections, freedom of speech, and access to political leaders. In each of these elements, campaign contributions had a damaging impact.

Given the fact that winning an election is highly correlated with donations, it is difficult to argue that we have free and fair elections in the US. Although people are free to express their views without (too much) fear of government reprisal, having one's voice actually heard by a politician is challenging—except with contributions. As such, freedom of speech is apparently not "free." In a similar vein, access to politicians typically only comes when a contribution is given—another way in which campaign contributions reduce the degree to which our system is truly democratic.

There have been some high-profile cases of bribery in recent decades. Members of the house such as Bob Ney, William Jefferson, Randall "Duke" Cunningham, and James Traficant faced indictments over their misdeeds, and all of them faced jail time. The Duke Cunningham and William Jefferson cases were especially egregious, each in their own way: Duke Cunningham essentially sold defense contracts to the highest bidders, and kept a price sheet that listed the amount of money he expected in exchange for defense contracts of X millions of dollars. William Jefferson was caught in a bribery sting with $90,000 in his possession—money he kept in his freezer.

Unlike with bribery, simply accepting campaign contributions—and even being influenced by said contributions—is not illegal. It is, however, a case of organizational deviance. Organizational deviance, as its name implies, involves organizations/entities, not just individuals. To be considered organizational deviance, actions need to meet four criteria: (1) they must go against external norms, (2) they must find support within the organization, (3) they must be known by those at the top, and (4) new members must be socialized into those same acts (Ermann and Lundman 1978). Every single one of these criteria is met when looking at campaign contributions and contributor influence. Donor influence is therefore a form of organizational deviance; it also creates institutional corruption.

Our political institutions and their members are subject to "competing dependencies" because of our campaign finance system. They are supposed to be dependent upon the people alone—the people who they are sworn to represent. Instead, because campaign contributions are critical to waging a successful (re)election campaign, political actors become dependent upon their donors as well—and they reward them handsomely via favorable policy. The result is that policy reflects the interests of the elite—donors—rather

Implications for our Democracy 83

than the interests of the people (Gilens and Page 2014). Sometimes this influence can verge on the criminal.

State-corporate crime involves "illegal or socially injurious actions that result from a mutually reinforcing interaction between (1) policies and/or practices in pursuit of the goals of one or more institutions of political governance and (2) policies and/or practices in pursuit of the goals of one or more institutions of economic production and distribution" (Aulette and Michalowski 1993:175). As noted in Chapter 5 as well as this chapter, we saw this with the Gramm-Leach-Bliley Act of 1999 and the Commodity Futures Modernization Act of 2000. These bills led to the housing crisis and the Great Recession, costing millions of people their houses and jobs—and campaign contributions had a significant effect on the passage of these bills.

Taken together, it is clear that campaign contributions and their influence have an adverse impact on our democracy. Indeed, it may no longer be appropriate to refer to our system as a democracy. Instead, our system looks much more like an oligarchy or plutocracy. Rather than having a political system in which the people rule, we have a system in which a small group of well-funded donors rule. Scholars such as G. William Domhoff (1967, 2014) have argued for decades that a wealthy upper class rules America, and they are right. As more and more evidence adds up, it is clear that donations influence policy (e.g. Peoples 2010, Roscoe and Jenkins 2005, Stratmann 2005) and that political decisions reflect the interests of "the elite" rather than "the people" (e.g. Gilens and Page 2014). Our democratic republic has lost its way (Lessig 2011)—*it has become an oligarchy/plutocracy.* How do we get our democracy back? The final chapter of this book will propose some solutions that, if implemented, could help restore our democracy and rid us of the plutocracy that has taken over our nation. First, though, the next chapter will discuss the implications of these findings for theories of power structure.

References

Aulette, Judy Root and Raymond Michalowski. 1993. "Fire in Hamlet: A Case Study of a State-Corporate Crime." Pp. 171–206 in *Political Crime in Contemporary America: A Critical Approach*, edited by Kenneth D. Tunnell. New York: Garland.

Bennett, William Finn. 2005. "Yacht 'Duke Stir' Owned by Defense Contractor Docked at Cunningham's Slip." *North County Times.* https://web. archive.org/web/20091211200540/www.nctimes.com/news/local/ article_28fa2fe2-613a-55cb-853b-80b59cc5f571.html

84 *Implications for our Democracy*

Bump, Philip. 2016. "There Have Been Just Four Documented Cases of Voter Fraud in the 2016 Election." *The Washington Post.* www.washingtonpost. com/news/the-fix/wp/2016/12/01/0-000002-percent-of-all-the-ballots-cast-in-the-2016-election-were-fraudulent/?noredirect=on&utm_term=. 18b6e8402c4d

Chambliss, William J. 1989. "State-Organized Crime—The American Society of Criminology, 1988 Presidential Address." *Criminology* 27:183–208.

CNN. 2002. "Traficant Guilty of Bribery, Racketeering." *CNN.com/ LAWcenter.* www.cnn.com/2002/LAW/04/11/traficant.trial/

Condon, George E. Jr. 2014. "Disgraced Congressman Randy 'Duke' Cunningham Is a Free Man Again." *The Atlantic.* www.theatlantic. com/politics/archive/2014/07/disgraced-congressman-randy-duke-cunningham-is-a-free-man-again/442878/

Domhoff, G. William. 1967. *Who Rules America?* Englewood Cliffs, NJ: Prentice Hall.

Domhoff, G. William. 2014. *Who Rules America? The Triumph of the Corporate Rich.* 7th Ed. New York: McGraw-Hill.

Dugan, Andrew. 2015. "Majority of Americans See Congress as Out of Touch, Corrupt." Gallup. https://news.gallup.com/poll/185918/ majority-americans-congress-touch-corrupt.aspx

Ermann, M. David and Richard J. Lundman. 1978. "Deviant Acts by Complex Organizations: Deviance and Social Control at the Organizational Level of Analysis." *The Sociological Quarterly* 19:55–67.

Gallup. 2019. "Congress and the Public." *Gallup.* https://news.gallup.com/ poll/1600/congress-public.aspx

Gilens, Martin, and Benjamin I. Page. 2014. "Testing Theories of American Politics: Elites, Interest Groups, and Average Citizens." *Perspectives on Politics* 12:564–581.

Helderman, Rosalind S., Matt Zapotosky, and Devlin Barrett. 2018. "Cohen's Claim about Trump May Spark Calls for Impeachment but is Unlikely to Lead to Charges." *The Washington Post.* www.washingtonpost. com/world/national-security/cohens-claim-about-trump-may-spark-calls-for-impeachment-but-is-unlikely-to-lead-to-charges/ 2018/08/21/4e432aec-a167-11e8-93e3-24d1703d2a7a_story.html?nore direct=on&utm_term=.76efb7ab4b55

Kaiser, Robert G. 2009. *So Damn Much Money: The Triumph of Lobbying and the Corrosion of American Government.* New York: Knopf.

Lengel, Allan. 2006. "FBI Says Jefferson Was Filmed Taking Cash Affidavit Details Sting on Lawmaker." *Washington Post.* www.washingtonpost. com/archive/politics/2006/05/22/fbi-says-jefferson-was-filmed-taking-cash-span-classbankheadaffidavit-details-sting-on-lawmakerspan/6bf 27a8c-34cb-421b-8862-a824013535a4/?noredirect=on&utm_term=. d6c5322ff178

Lessig, Lawrence. 2011. *Republic, Lost: How Money Corrupts Congress—and a Plan to Stop It.* New York: Twelve.

Lessig, Lawrence. 2013. "Foreword: 'Institutional Corruption' Defined." *Journal of Law, Medicine and Ethics* 41:553–555.

Mayer, William G. 2001. "Public Attitudes on Campaign Finance." Pp. 47–69 in *A User's Guide to Campaign Finance Reform*, edited by Gerald C. Lubenow. Lanham, MD: Rowman & Littlefield.

Nash, J. 2008. "Ney Freed after Serving 17 Months for Corruption." *Columbus Dispatch*. www.dispatch.com/content/stories/local/2008/08/16/NEYOUT.ART_ART_08-16-08_B4_RSB1SV9.html

Peoples, Clayton D. 2010. "Contributor Influence in Congress: Social Ties and PAC Effects on U.S. House Policymaking." *The Sociological Quarterly* 51:649–677.

Peoples, Clayton D. and James E. Sutton. 2015. "Congressional Bribery as State-Corporate Crime: A Social Network Analysis." *Crime, Law, and Social Change* 64:103–125.

Public Policy Polling. 2013. "Congress Somewhere below Cockroaches, Traffic Jams, and Nickelback in Americans' Esteem." www.publicpolicy polling.com/main/2013/01/congress-somewhere-below-cockroaches-traffic-jams-and-nickleback-in-americans-esteem.html

Roscoe, Douglas D. and Shannon Jenkins. 2005. "A Meta-Analysis of Campaign Contributions' Impact on Roll Call Voting." *Social Science Quarterly* 86:52–68.

Ross, Jeffrey Ian. 2015. "Controlling State Crime and Alternative Reactions." Pp. 492–502 in *The Routledge International Handbook of Crimes of the Powerful*, edited by Greg Barak. New York: Routledge.

Schram, Martin. 1995. "Speaking Freely: Former Members of Congress Talk about Money in Politics." Washington, D.C.: Center for Responsive Politics.

Stern, Marcus. 2005. "Lawmaker's Home Sale Questioned." *San Diego Tribune*. http://legacy.sandiegouniontribune.com/news/politics/20050612-9999-1n12windfall.html

Stratmann, Thomas. 2005. "Some Talk: Money in Politics. A (Partial) Review of the Literature." *Public Choice* 124:135–156.

Thrush, Glenn. 2018. "Mulvaney, Watchdog Bureau's Leader, Advises Bankers on Ways to Curtail Agency." *New York Times*. www.nytimes.com/2018/04/24/us/mulvaney-consumer-financial-protection-bureau.html

US Attorney. 2018. Charges Filed Against Michael Cohen in the Southern District of New York.

US Department of Justice. 2006. "Former Lobbyist Jack Abramoff Pleads Guilty to Charges Involving Corruption, Fraud Conspiracy, and Tax Evasion." www.justice.gov/archive/opa/pr/2006/January/06_crm_002.html

Weiser, Benjamin and William K. Rashbaum. 2018. "Michael Cohen Sentenced to 3 Years After Implicating Trump in Hush-Money Scandal." *New York Times*. www.nytimes.com/2018/12/12/nyregion/michael-cohen-sentence-trump.html

7 Implications for Theories of Power Structure

As Chapters 4 through 6 clearly demonstrate, campaign contributions have implications for the real world. Donations put the economy at risk, increase inequality, and undermine democracy. Campaign contributions also have implications for theorizing and scholarship on political matters.

For many decades, scholars have debated the role of power in politics. Out of these debates have emerged three competing theoretical perspectives that offer very different views of our political system: pluralist theory, elite-power theory (also known as class-dominance theory), and state-centered theory (more recently dubbed "institutionalist theory"). They are each discussed in turn below.

Three Main Theories of Power Structure

Pluralist Theory

Pluralist theory is rooted in ideal conceptions of democracy. It argues that (a) our political system is largely open to people's input and that (b) no one particular group of people exerts outsize influence. Pluralist theory was quite popular in the post-World War II era of the 1950s and early 1960s, and reflected a peachy view of society in which the conflicts of the past were behind us and society and its institutions (e.g. the political system) were well balanced and worked for the majority of the populace.

Pluralist theory is anchored in the work of Robert Dahl, a Yale political scientist who produced an oft-cited study of power structure in New Haven, CT. In his study, Dahl (1961) looked at the major players in decision-making in New Haven as well as how they made their decisions. He contended that the power structure in New Haven reflected an ideal pluralist arrangement. In his assessment, New Haven's political scene was open to input from society and there was no single, powerful core of leaders dominating decisions. Dahl's study was not without controversy—for instance, Domhoff (1978) conducted his own study of New Haven and found that New Haven in fact had a powerful core of leaders—but it nonetheless served as a foundation for the pluralist perspective.

Over the years, pluralism began to shift its focus away from its community power foundations à la Dahl (1961) and move into the realm of public opinion. In the 1980s and 1990s, a flurry of scholarship coalesced around this theme, much of it spearheaded by Paul Burstein at the University of Washington (e.g. Burstein 1998). The basic argument forwarded by Burstein is that it is not just at the community level in which people are able to impact decisions. Even at the federal level, he contends, the government is responsive to public opinion on issues, and politicians pay attention to the views of their constituents and the general public when making decisions on policy. Interestingly, Burstein eventually reevaluated his claims and acknowledged that public opinion may not be as impactful as he once thought (Burstein 2006). Despite the adjustment in his position, his work nonetheless helped shift the focus of pluralism toward the federal level and public opinion.

Elite-Power Theory ("Class-Dominance")

Elite-power theory offers a rebuttal to pluralism and contends that while our system may be open to input, it is only the powerful— those with money and the elite—who have a significant influence. From this viewpoint, it is primarily the wealthy upper class and members of the business community who affect policy; everyone else is largely ignored by politicians. This perspective gained popularity in the mid- to late 1960s as social movements (e.g. Civil Rights, antiwar) became visible and social unrest seemed the norm. But some of the most important works bolstering elite-power theory were published in the 1950s.

There is not one single work that serves as a foundation for elite-power theory, but, instead, there are numerous studies that serve as anchors. The first of these studies was conducted by Floyd Hunter, a sociologist who taught at the University of North Carolina before moving to California. In his study, Hunter (1953) examined power structure in Atlanta, GA and found that there was a rather small network of powerful individuals who made most of the important decisions for the city. (Dahl's 1961 study of New Haven can be viewed as a response to Hunter's study of Atlanta, albeit in a different city.)

88 *Implications for Power Structure*

After the publication of Hunter's (1953) study of Atlanta, C. Wright Mills, a well-known Columbia sociologist, offered an analysis of power structure at the national level. In his study, which resulted in the book *The Power Elite*, Mills (1956) argued that some of the same principles that Hunter expounded in Atlanta applied to the national power structure as well. In essence, Mills asserted that there is a small core of powerful leaders who make decisions for the country. This core of leaders is made up of individuals whose occupations put them at the top of the economic, political, and military spheres of society, such as corporate CEOs, the President, and Generals.

Following C. Wright Mills's work on the power elite, G. William Domhoff, a well-known sociologist based at the University of California in Santa Cruz, offered his own analysis of power structure at the national level, culminating in multiple editions of a top sociology monograph, *Who Rules America?* Although Domhoff (1967) generally agrees with Mills that there is a powerful core of decision-makers in the US, he departs from Mills on where this power comes from. For Mills, as above, power is mainly concentrated within positions (e.g. the office of the presidency); for Domhoff, however, power is more fluid, and is the result of networks, money, and influence. Domhoff ultimately argues that the wealthy upper class shapes the important decisions of our day through policy formation groups, think tanks, and other means (e.g. campaign contributions) rather than through securing the top decision-making posts, as Mills posited.

Taken together, the works of Hunter (1953), Mills (1956), and Domhoff (1967) provide anchors for the elite-power perspective. Although these works differ slightly in scale (e.g. community, à la Hunter; versus national, à la Mills and Domhoff), they all contend that we do *not* have a pluralist system. Instead, they argue, we have a system in which power is concentrated in the hands of a few in the business and political sectors of society—the "power elite," to use Mills's language.

Elite-power theory underwent some changes since its foundations in the 1950s and 1960s. For instance, a debate occurred in the 1970s between "instrumentalists" (Miliband 1969) and "structuralists" (Poulantzas 1974). Instrumentalists argued that elites and powerful entities have a direct impact on policy; structuralists, on the other hand, contended that much of this influence is indirect in that policymakers will support business interests by default in capitalist systems.

Implications for Power Structure   89

State-Centered Theory ("Institutionalism")

The instrumentalist versus structuralist debate—particularly the arguments of structuralism—is part of what led to the development of state-centered theory. State-centered theory makes the case that our political system is relatively closed. It contends that neither "the people" (e.g. constituents, the public) nor elites (e.g. contributors and lobbyists) have a great influence on the important decisions of our day. Instead, it argues, policy is simply a reflection of the wishes of state actors themselves—the politicians and bureaucrats who are in a position to write and enforce laws.

As noted above, state-centered theory emerged in the late 1970s in response to the debates between pluralist and elite-power theory. Part of what spurred the development of state-centered theory was an argument in the late 1970s that "the ruling class does not rule" (Block 1977). Despite the fact that elites tend to get the policy they want, it is merely a coincidence according to this view. It argues that state actors will pass certain policies *independent* of elite influence.

Following the contention that the ruling class does not rule (Block 1977), state-centered theory took off in the late 1970s and through the 1980s, fueled by the work of Theda Skocpol (e.g. 1979) at Harvard University and her protégés (e.g. Amenta and Parikh 1989). Early state-centered theory argued that state actors are largely autonomous in their decision-making powers. Since then, though, state-centered theory has adjusted its claims. It has shifted toward a greater focus on governmental institutions rather than state actors themselves, hence the new name "institutionalism." It nonetheless retains its core position that entities outside the state typically have little/no influence on governmental decisions—but it has moderated to allow that sometimes perhaps outsiders can have a little impact.

Testing Theories of Power Structure

As noted above, pluralist, elite-power, and state-centered theories have changed a bit over time. The challenge with this is that they have become somewhat "watered down" versions of their previous positions. As a result, they are virtually indistinguishable on the key dimensions that at one time actually made them distinct, competing theories; it is therefore difficult to test the theories given that their arguments are so similar. As such, I would contend that a return to some of their original, more distinct arguments is warranted (Peoples 2009), which allows for empirical testing to answer the

90   *Implications for Power Structure*

question, "Which theory best explains the power structure in the US?" Numerous empirical tests have been done over the years to try to answer this question. These tests generally fall into two categories: case studies and empirical studies. Empirical studies, then, can be further subdivided based on what is examined: policy influence versus actual policy outcomes (e.g. who wins).

Case Studies

Case studies are exactly what the name implies: studies of specific cases. Case studies can be useful for testing theories of power structure research in that one can look at a specific case—say the New Deal—and analyze the extent to which various interest groups, if any, had influence on the policy. One of the pros of case studies is that they can provide great detail; case studies are lacking, however, in that they do not produce generalizable results.

Not surprisingly, case studies sometimes produce mixed results for the power structure debates. Take research on community power structure, for instance. As noted already, work by Hunter (1953) on Atlanta shows that there is a relatively fixed power structure in which certain key players dominate community decision-making. Research by Dahl (1961), however, suggests that the same may not be true of New Haven. But later research by Domhoff (1978) calls this into question and shows that power in New Haven is far more fixed than Dahl contended.

Case studies of the New Deal yield similarly mixed findings. There was a blossoming of work and commentary in the 1980s on the New Deal (e.g. Amenta and Parikh 1989; Jenkins and Brents 1989; Levine 1988; Quadagno 1984; Skocpol and Amenta 1985). Some of these studies show significant influence of the corporate class on New Deal policies such as the Social Security Act (e.g. Jenkins and Brents 1989; Levine 1988); others, however, counter that the corporate class "did not want the Social Security Act" (Amenta and Parikh 1989:124) and that New Deal legislation was opposed by "virtually all politically active" members of the corporate class (Skocpol and Amenta 1985:572). But more recent archival research demonstrates that some of the most important policies coming out of the New Deal—the Social Security Act, the Agricultural Adjustment Act, and the National Labor Relations Act—were in fact proposed by corporate moderates in the north (Domhoff and Webber 2011), which refutes the claims of earlier work by Amenta and Skocpol.

Implications for Power Structure 91

One realm of work that does not produce such mixed findings is scholarship looking into transportation issues in California. Research shows that business interests worked together on the planning of public transportation routes in California in the 1960s and 1970s (Whitt 1982). Although these businesses did not always favor the plans (e.g. routes, etc.), they nonetheless worked alongside one another in approving the policies and shaping the ultimate outcomes.

Although it is possible to have a set of case studies that result in consistent findings, as with work on California transportation issues (Whitt 1982), many studies (e.g. community power structure and the New Deal) have produced mixed findings. These divergent results leave some questions unanswered, including the most important question of all: "Which theory best explains power structure in the US?" To answer this with greater clarity, we need to look at empirical studies.

Empirical Research

Empirical research refers to work that relies on statistics to reach its conclusions. Consequently, empirical research is usually quantitative in nature rather than qualitative. This means that, unlike case studies, empirical studies do *not* provide rich detail but *do* provide generalizable results. Generalizability is what is needed to truly answer the question of which theory best explains power in the US, so empirical research provides a far clearer picture than case studies alone.

Empirical studies that examine power structure in the US can be divided into two main types according to *what*, specifically, they look at: (1) influence on policy and (2) actual policy outcomes. Although these are related topics, there are important distinctions between the two. For instance, it could be that certain interests (e.g. business PACs) are able to influence how lawmakers vote on bills, but this does not necessarily mean that those interests get the outcomes they desire. To know this, we have to look at actual policy outcomes and see who gets what they want over time (in other words, who "wins"). It is actually the combination of the two— influence and outcomes—that would tell the whole story. After all, as noted earlier, there are some who would argue that despite the corporate class frequently getting what they want, they are not actually in control of the process (Block 1977; Poulantzas 1974; Skocpol 1979)—in other words, they do not have much actual *influence*. Finding evidence of both favorable policy outcomes *and* influence would refute those claims.

92 *Implications for Power Structure*

Special Interest Influence

In terms of specific special interests and their influence, one good test is to compare business and labor. Both entities are very active in politics. Indeed, business and labor combined contribute more than 50 percent of the PAC money going to winning House candidates. Moreover, business and labor are not typically on the same side of issues. This likely stems from their different position in relation to the means of production.

Dating back to the classical economic works of Adam Smith and David Ricardo, it has been understood that much of where profit in capitalism comes from is paying workers less than the value of their labor—an insight referred to as the "labor theory of value" or the "surplus value theory of labor." According to Karl Marx, owners of the means of production (e.g. business owners) and non-owners (workers) are the two main players in this equation and represent the two main classes in capitalism—classes that have opposing economic interests. Their opposition to one another can manifest in a number of different ways, depending on the setting. For instance, in the workplace, it may take the form of a labor strike or business-initiated lockout of workers. In the political arena, though, it could manifest as support for opposing candidates or different issue positions. Campaign contributions reflect this opposition quite well.

As shown in Chapter 2, business PACs tend to follow a "pragmatic" strategy of giving to the candidate who is expected to win (or both candidates in the close race), and give generously to candidates of both parties; labor PACs, on the other hand, follow an "ideological" strategy of giving to candidates who appear to support labor and its causes—more often democratic candidates than republicans. This leads to a disparity in business giving versus labor giving: business tends to donate to viable candidates across the aisle, while labor tends to contribute to a narrower field of allies. In short, business PACs and labor PACs donate in very different ways. But what about the impact of their donations?

Pluralist theory would posit that business and labor contributions ought to have a similar, detectable influence on policy. As noted earlier, pluralism contends that a variety of groups not only vie for influence, but ultimately achieve some success. It is the ideal view of democracy in which a wide array of interests have political sway. Elite-power theory (or class dominance), on the other hand, would argue that business has more influence than labor. After all, according to this theory, it is a small segment of society that ultimately influences policy. Finally, state-centered theory (or institutionalism) would forward the case that neither business nor labor should have any significant influence on policy. If it is primarily state actors who drive policy decisions, not special interests, then the effect of business or labor contributions should be negligible.

Examining business and labor contributions, I conducted research with a student about a decade ago that showed that business contributions had a significant influence on policy voting in the 105th US House (1997–98) while labor did not (Peoples and Gortari 2008). In a more comprehensive analysis on multiple Houses over time (eight Houses totaling sixteen years), I found a similar pattern: over the period, only business contributions had a consistently significant influence on policy; labor had some influence, but it was only intermittent (Peoples 2007). These results fail to support the state-centered view since outside entities had a significant influence on policy. The results also fail to support pluralism given that labor did not have nearly the same influence as business. Instead, elite-power/class-dominance theory is best supported by these findings. But what about policy outcomes?

Who Wins?

When looking at whose policy preferences are best reflected in the legislation that is passed/enacted—in essence, looking at who wins—the logic is similar to the work (above) comparing business and labor influence: pluralist theory would posit that both elites and the general public get their way; elite-power theory would argue that elites see their preferences favored over the preferences of the general public; and state-centered theory would contend that there should be no difference—in other words, if policy happens to support the preferences of one group over another, it would just be by chance, and would not translate across a large number of bills.

The work of Gilens and Page (2014) is very relevant here. In their study, they look at whose interest is most reflected in policy outcomes, elites or the public. What they find is striking: "[Regression] analysis indicates that economic elites and organized groups representing business interests have substantial independent impacts on U.S. government policy, while average citizens and mass-based interest groups have little or no independent influence" (p. 564). What their study suggests is that policy ultimately reflects the interests of just a small percentage of Americans—an outcome that would be very much predicted by the elite-power/class-dominance camp, but not others.

94 *Implications for Power Structure*

Summary of Empirical Results

Taken together, the empirical findings highlighted above point toward elite-power/class-dominance theory being the best explanation of the power structure in the US. The findings on "who wins" seem to rule out pluralist theory. Given that elites tend to get what they want while other groups (e.g. the general public) do not, there is little/no evidence to support pluralist theory. That leaves elite-power theory and state-centered theory as possible explanations.

Although the fact that elites tend to win would seem to support elite-power theory, state-centered theorists could counter that this is merely a coincidence. Put differently, perhaps elites win because state actors and entities want the policies—not necessarily because elites want them. This is where the findings on policy influence are especially helpful.

Given that business PACs impact policymaking while labor PACs do not, this seems to refute state-centered theory as a viable explanation. There should be no statistical relationship between the receipt of campaign contributions and roll call votes if the votes have nothing to do with donor influence. Because there is a statistically significant relationship, there is strong evidence in support of elite-power/class-dominance theory (and no evidence to support state-centered theory). Moreover, the instrumentalism of Miliband (1969) finds more support in these findings than the structuralism of Poulantzas (1974).

Ultimately, the findings concerning policy influence combined with results on "who wins" provide strong evidence that elite-power/class-dominance theory is the best explanation for the power structure in the US. Pluralist theory is not supported by either area of research. Because elites and businesses both influence policy decisions and get what they want, whereas the public and labor unions do not, pluralist theory is not supported at all. Moreover, state-centered theory finds very little support across the two areas. Although one might be able to claim that elites getting what they want does not necessarily rule out state-centered theory, the fact that business PACs have a direct influence on roll call voting shows that their "winning" in the policy realm is no coincidence: they actively influence lawmakers to pass and implement these favorable policies. Elite-power/class-dominance theory best explains these patterns.

Discussion

Combined with insights from other chapters of the book, the findings highlighted in this chapter paint a grim picture of the current state of our society in the US. Rather than having a democratic system in which the wishes of the people are well-represented in policy decisions, we instead have an oligarchy in which the wishes of businesses and the elite are represented while others are largely ignored. Although it would be great to imagine that the impacts of this are benign, evidence suggests otherwise.

The interests of businesses and the elite are not always the best interests of society. Their influence can create and exacerbate inequality through government contracts, subsidies, and the tax code. In short, well-positioned individuals and businesses win, and the rich get richer; everyone else remains stagnant or becomes poorer. This widening of the gap between the rich and the poor is already problematic; the impact on the economy, though, can be catastrophic.

Because businesses and elites have disproportionate sway over decisions related to economic exchange, they can impact policy in their favor—even when it puts the health of the economy at risk. The perfect example of this was the Financial Crisis and associated Great Recession. Businesses and the elite influenced the passage of bills that allowed banking and investing firms to merge *and* permitted the virtually unregulated sale of risky derivatives. As the housing bubble burst, these derivatives rapidly dropped in value, and firms that insured them or had too many derivatives on their books faced closure. This downward spiral led to the Financial Crisis and ensuing Great Recession, costing the economy up to $14trillion in value and leading millions of people to lose their jobs and their homes.

Given the significant role of campaign contributions in all of the above, it is clear that our current campaign finance system is detrimental to our democracy, our economy, and our society as a whole. It should therefore be reformed to limit the damage it inflicts on our institutions. The final chapter of the book—Chapter 8—will propose a number of different campaign finance reforms. Additionally, it will propose a variety of ways in which reform can be accomplished.

References

Amenta, Edwin and Sunita Parikh. 1989. "Capitalists Did Not Want the Social Security Act: A Critique of the 'Capitalist Dominance' Thesis." *American Sociological Review* 55:124–129.

Block, Fred. 1977. "The Ruling Class Does Not Rule: Notes on the Marxist Theory of the State." *Socialist Revolution* 7:6–28.

Burstein, Paul. 1998. "Bringing the Public Back In: Should Sociologists Consider the Impact of Public Opinion on Public Policy?" *Social Forces* 77:27–62.

96 *Implications for Power Structure*

Burstein, Paul. 2006. "Why Estimates of the Impact of Public Opinion on Public Policy Are Too High: Empirical and Theoretical Implications." *Social Forces* 84: 2273–2290.

Dahl, Robert. 1961. *Who Governs?* New Haven, CT: Yale University Press.

Domhoff, G. William. 1967. *Who Rules America?* Englewood Cliffs, NJ: Prentice Hall.

Domhoff, G. William. 1978. *Who Really Rules? New Haven and Community Power Reexamined.* New Brunswick, NJ: Transaction.

Domhoff, G. William and Michael J. Webber. 2011. *Class and Power in the New Deal: Corporate Moderates, Southern Democrats, and the Liberal-Labor Coalition.* Palo Alto, CA: Stanford University Press.

Gilens, Martin, and Benjamin I. Page. 2014. "Testing Theories of American Politics: Elites, Interest Groups, and Average Citizens." *Perspectives on Politics* 12:564–581.

Hunter, Floyd. 1953. *Community Power Structure.* Chapel Hill, NC: University of North Carolina Press.

Jenkins, J. Craig and Barbara Brents. 1989. "Social Protest, Hegemonic Competition, and Social Reform: A Political Struggle Interpretation of the Origins of the American Welfare State." *American Sociological Review* 54:891–909.

Levine, Rhonda F. 1988. *Class Struggle and the New Deal: Industrial Labor, Industrial Capital, and the State.* Lawrence, KS: University of Kansas Press.

Miliband, Ralph. 1969. *The State in Capitalist Society.* London: Weidenfeld & Nicolson.

Mills, C. Wright. 1956. *The Power Elite.* New York: Oxford University Press.

Peoples, Clayton D. 2007. "Class Dominance and Policymaking in the U.S. House: Why 'Who Rules' is Right after Forty Years." *Annual Meeting of the Pacific Sociological Association.* Oakland, CA.

Peoples, Clayton D. 2009. "Reviving Power Structure Research: Present Problems, their Solutions, and Future Directions." *Political Power and Social Theory* 20:3–38.

Peoples, Clayton D. and Michael Gortari. 2008. "The Impact of Campaign Contributions on Policymaking in the U.S. and Canada: Theoretical and Public Policy Implications." *Research in Political Sociology* 17:43–64.

Poulantzas, Nicos. 1974. *Political Power and Social Classes.* London: New Left Books.

Quadagno, Jill S. 1984. "Welfare Capitalism and the Social Security Act of 1935." *American Sociological Review* 49:632–647.

Skocpol, Theda. 1979. *States and Social Revolutions: A Comparative Analysis of France, Russia, and China.* Cambridge: Cambridge University Press.

Skocpol, Theda and Edwin Amenta. 1985. "Did Capitalists Shape Social Security?" *American Sociological Review* 52:572–575.

Whitt, J. Allen. 1982. *Urban Elites and Mass Transportation: The Dialectics of Power.* Princeton University Press.

8 Political Reform

As the previous chapters demonstrate, our campaign finance system is flawed. It favors wealthy donors over average citizens. Policy reflects the interests of big contributors rather than the public-at-large. The consequences range from merely harmful to nearly catastrophic. Tax policy favors the rich over the poor; rules/regulations favor businesses over labor; and in some unique cases (e.g. the laws/policies that led to the Great Recession) contributions can bring our entire economy to the brink of collapse. In short, our current way of funding campaigns increases inequality, adversely impacts our economy, and undermines our democracy.

Some propose campaign finance reform as a solution to the above issues. The public favors this (Mayer 2001), and some scholars argue that the fate of our Republic is contingent upon such reform (Lessig 2011). But campaign finance reform is not the only option. Other reforms could help diminish the influence of money in politics without drastically changing the campaign finance system. All of these options are discussed in turn in this chapter.

The chapter begins with campaign finance reform, and outlines four categories of such reform, in increasing order of magnitude: (1) increasing transparency/disclosure, (2) limiting contributions, (3) making contributions anonymous to recipients, and (4) eliminating private contributions altogether. The chapter then turns to other reforms, such as changing the policymaking process, closing the revolving door, and reducing conflicts of interest. Finally, the chapter discusses *how* these reforms might become reality before offering some concluding remarks.

Campaign Finance Reform

Transparency/Disclosure

Some would argue that more transparency and disclosure is all we need to ensure that contributions do not cause harm. But disclosure

98   *Political Reform*

has been referred to as the "do-little" approach (Goidel et al. 1999), and for good reason—it does very little to reform the system we presently have. Lessig (2011) makes this point quite clear by describing it as a "reform that won't reform" (p. 251).

The notion that transparency/disclosure would solve our campaign finance woes makes very narrow assumptions about how contributions impact our system. This perspective effectively argues that contributions do not influence policy—or if they do, said influence is not harmful—and instead simply contends that the primary issue is one of simple disclosure. By this logic, if all contributions were fully disclosed, no problems would exist in our system. This is incorrect on a number of counts.

First, simply disclosing contributions would not allow the average citizen to see the connection between the contributions, politicians, and policy. Most people are unfamiliar with social network analysis (SNA) and are therefore unable to "connect the dots" that link contributors, lobbyists, and politicians. Moreover, most people lack the training in statistics that would allow them to assess whether or not a significant relationship exists between contributions and votes. In short, while transparency is important, it is not a panacea. Just as access to coding languages would not enable most people to become expert programmers, access to campaign finance data would not allow most people to properly assess contribution influence.

Second, we already have disclosure. Only very specific kinds of contributions today lack full disclosure—SuperPAC contributions. Individual contributions and PAC contributions are already fully disclosed and are available to the public via both the FEC as well as other data compilers (e.g. Center for Responsive Politics, MapLight). So disclosure isn't really reform—it's just tweaking what we already have.

Third, and perhaps most importantly, the types of contributions that are already fully disclosed have a significant influence on lawmaking *despite* the fact that they are disclosed. Look at PAC contributions: PAC contributions are fully disclosed, yet PAC contributions have a consistent, statistically significant influence on policy (Peoples 2010; Roscoe and Jenkins 2005; Stratmann 2005). This suggests that simple disclosure/transparency would not diminish the impact of contributions, because it hasn't thus far in the many years in which we have had transparency.

Increasing transparency would clearly have little impact on our existing campaign finance system. Donors would still contribute as they do already, and access and/or influence would continue. Other types of reform are needed to result in real change. One possibility is to place stricter limits on campaign contributions.

Stricter Limits

Limiting contributions could take on any number of different forms given that contributions are allowed from multiple sources—SuperPACs, PACs, and individuals—and are currently allowed in varying amounts from each of those sources. In the below paragraphs, I address these themes and provide a basic overview of the many different ways in which contributions could be limited beyond current regulations (see Chapter 2 for more detail on current limits).

In terms of sources, limits could be placed on SuperPAC contributions and other "soft" donations, which are virtually unregulated and unlimited. Recall that this was the logic behind the Bipartisan Campaign Reform Act (BCRA) of 2002. Although the BCRA was ultimately struck down by the Supreme Court's *Citizens United* decision, one could make the case that new restrictions are needed on these kinds of contributions now that we have a better sense of what contributions look like in the post-*Citizens-United* world.

Restrictions on SuperPACs could take a couple of forms: (1) the amount of money allowed from SuperPACs could be limited, or (2) SuperPACs could be outlawed entirely. The former scenario seems more likely to hold up to judicial scrutiny given the aforementioned decision in *Citizens United*. But as alluded to above, one could contend that when the Supreme Court handed down its *Citizens United* decision, it was unknown how the campaign finance landscape would evolve and change in response. Now that we have had numerous election cycles since *Citizens United*, we have a better handle on how SuperPACs operate. Given that contributions have skyrocketed in the post-*Citizens-United* era, one could argue that new restrictions are in order—and that a new examination by the courts, should it come to that, would be warranted.

A second option is that limits could be placed on PAC contributions. Although PAC contributions are already restricted in certain ways, there is certainly room to further limit them. As noted already, PACs are effectively interest groups. As such, one could make the case that a way to reduce the influence of special interests in politics would be to restrict PAC contributions further. It is unclear how the courts would treat such restrictions. But the

100 *Political Reform*

case could be made that if individuals are still allowed to contribute to campaigns in other ways (e.g. via individual contributions), restricting PAC contributions would not hinder free speech—a big concern of the Supreme Court. Under current laws, individuals can contribute to campaigns via PACs, but are also free to contribute directly as individuals. But perhaps individual contributions could/should be restricted as well.

As already noted in Chapter 2, there are currently restrictions on individual contributions—restrictions that have held up in the courts. For instance, while the *McCutcheon* decision raised the overall total limits on individual contributions, other restrictions were upheld. For instance, donors are limited to contributions of $2,700 per candidate, per election. Since these limits were not weakened by the Supreme Court, it is possible that the amount could be restricted further without fear of the court overturning such a move. This would bring us closer to what some refer to as "small-dollar" financing of campaigns.

Small-Dollar Financing

Small-dollar financing is the idea that political campaigns ought to be funded by a wide array of contributors, all of whom donate relatively small amounts, rather than a small group of donors who contribute large sums. By enacting stricter regulations (e.g. lowering allowable amounts to hundreds of dollars, rather than thousands), we would effectively move toward small-dollar financing. This might help resolve the issue of "big money" in politics.

In theory, small dollar financing would level the playing field and increase the political clout of everyday citizens who may wish to donate but cannot contribute the thousands that well-resourced individuals or PACs can. Yet as noted by Ansolabehere et al. (2003), very few PACs today contribute the maximum allowable amounts ($5,000 per candidate per election). Plus, my own work shows that money amount, per se, matters less than the social ties between contributors and lawmakers (Peoples 2010). So limiting contribution amounts may have less impact than one would imagine. Anonymizing contributions, however, would likely have a significant impact.

Anonymous Contributions

Today, lawmakers know who their contributors are. As noted earlier, contributors often give in person to establish/maintain their

Political Reform 101

friendships with lawmakers (Clawson et al. 1998). This, in turn, leads quite directly to access and influence, as described in Chapter 3. But imagine a scenario in which lawmakers are blind to who is giving them money. This is exactly what Ackerman and Ayres (2004) propose, and it just might be what is needed to curb contribution influence. After all, if lawmakers don't know who has given them money, they would not feel an obligation to reciprocate via contracts, subsidies, tax code and/or regulatory changes, policy, etc.

Ackerman and Ayres (2004) construct an elaborate model through which campaign contributions would be anonymous. They build safeguards into their proposed system that would greatly diminish the likelihood that people could circumvent anonymity and gain leverage. Although no system can be foolproof—after all, there would still be incentive to tell a candidate that you support their campaign—it is nonetheless possible to devise a system that would render it difficult, if not impossible, for candidates to know who has given to whom. Yet as innovative as this idea is, one challenge is that it might end up working too well, if implemented.

Lessig (2011) points out that anonymizing contributions might have the unintended effect of drastically reducing campaign donations across the board. He points to a situation in Florida from the early 1970s to help illustrate this point: Statewide races for judicial posts in Florida briefly used an anonymous system of contributions, but the result was that "contributions dried up" (p. 262). In other words, if donors know that their contributions are anonymous—and, thus, would have less potential to lead to access and/or influence—they would likely reduce their contributions—or cease contributing altogether. Granted, this would not necessarily be a bad thing—indeed, one could argue that the ceasing of private donations to campaigns is exactly what we need to help restore our democracy. The difficulty is that it is expensive to wage a successful political campaign, as noted in Chapter 3 and elsewhere. Consequently, campaigns would have to be funded in some way. This is where public financing can come into play.

Public Financing

Whether a consequence of anonymous contributions or a reform in its own right, public financing of campaigns would effectively eliminate private donations, and, thus, truly alter the campaign finance landscape. Under a public financing system, politicians

102   *Political Reform*

would no longer feel an obligation to give something back to PACs and special interests because these entities would no longer be the source of their campaign funds. One could argue that this would be the optimal approach in the long term, as it would largely eliminate the influence of big donors while still ensuring that politicians are able to fund their campaigns. The challenge with this approach, though, is that it seems to fly in the face of the Supreme Court's stance that contributions are a form of free speech protected under the constitution, and could therefore be struck down in the courts. But there are some ways to (hopefully) circumvent this issue.

Probably the best way to get around the issue of limiting free speech is to allow the public to "opt in," should they desire. There are a couple ways of doing this. One option would be to simply allow people the choice of whether or not to allocate any of their tax dollars to the public financing of campaigns. This is what is already done with presidential elections. The second option would be to allow people to not only opt in, but, also, decide where their money goes (e.g. which party, which candidates). Each of these two options is discussed in more detail below.

When filling out your taxes, you may have noticed that there is a question, "Do you want $3 of your federal tax to go to the Presidential Election Campaign Fund?" with the options "yes" or "no." Although it is not very clear what that means, selecting "yes" would not change your tax liability (in other words, it would not add $3 to the amount you owe). Instead, selecting "yes" would simply reallocate $3 of your taxes to the Presidential Election Campaign Fund, which is a fund that presidential candidates can use, if they wish.

This Presidential Election Campaign Fund is a good idea, in principle; but it is set up in such a way that candidates, too, can decide whether or not to opt in, which limits its effectiveness. Under current policy, presidential candidates do not have to opt into the Presidential Election Campaign Fund; rather, they can choose to rely solely on private donations. Moreover, even those who do opt into the fund can supplement the fund with private donations—albeit with tighter restrictions. As a result, candidates rarely opt in—and when they do, they end up with less campaign cash than their opponents, as happened with John McCain in 2008. In short, the way the Presidential Election Campaign Fund is currently structured is not a true, public-financing-only system, and is therefore limited in its ability to result in real change in presidential elections. Moreover, it leaves out congressional elections entirely. Lessig (2011) proposes a possible solution to this.

Lessig (2011) argues for a blend of public financing and small-dollar for congressional elections. He calls his proposed system the "Grant and Franklin Project," referencing the characters that appear on the $50 bill (Ulysses Grant) and $100 bill (Benjamin Franklin). The reason why he references these specific dollar amounts is that he envisions that the first $50 someone contributes to the US Treasury in taxes (e.g. income taxes, etc.) could be converted into a "democracy voucher" that the person would contribute in whatever way they choose (e.g. favorite candidate, their registered party, an overall pot of funds, etc.); the person would also be allowed to donate up to $100 more out of their own pocket—again, however they choose—should they desire.

All the reforms mentioned above have pros and cons, but they are all likely better than doing nothing (perhaps with the exception of increasing disclosure, which does virtually nothing anyway). But campaign finance reform is likely not the only way to lessen the impact of campaign contributions. There may other reforms that could help limit the impact of political donations. A few possibilities are discussed below.

Other Reforms

Change the Policymaking Process

As noted in Chapter 4, Jones and Keiser (1987) find that contributions have the greatest impact on "low-visibility" bills. This is due, in part, to a strategy PAC officers and lobbyists use: they often sneak provisions into bills—perhaps even bills unrelated to the provisions—so that kickbacks and special deals remain hidden to all but a handful of individuals (Clawson et al. 1998). Infamous lobbyist Jack Abramoff readily admitted to such tactics in an interview with CBS News: "So what we did was we crafted language that was so obscure, so confusing, so uninformative, but so precise to change the U.S. code" (Abramoff 2012). Indeed, one of the preferred ways of doing this is to sneak provisions into a popular bill—ideally a reform bill. (Yes, you read that right: special provisions and earmarks are sometimes inserted into bills that purport to be about reform!)

104 *Political Reform*

How can we battle back against the above practices? There are a few possibilities, all having to do with process: (1) only allow single-issue legislation, (2) limit bill size and/or bill numbers, and (3) employ a team of independent experts to assess legislation and its impact before final votes/implementation.

Single-Issue Legislation

Single-issue legislation is exactly what it sounds like—legislation that is limited to a single issue or policy area. As noted earlier, at the federal level we do not have single-issue legislation. Instead, bills are complicated monstrosities pieced together like Frankenstein's beast. In some states, however, legislatures are bound to construct only single-issue legislation. This could potentially be duplicated at the federal level. Doing so could help reduce the impact of contributions and lobbyists.

The value of single-issue legislation is that it prevents donors and lobbyists from getting provisions inserted in bills that have nothing to do with the larger piece of legislation. This is important, because, as above, this is often how they sneak things into bills "under the radar." Granted, this would not diminish contributor influence altogether, as they would still likely seek to sway single-issue legislation that is of interest to them. But it would nonetheless prevent them from sneaking things into bills where they do not belong.

Bill Size/Number Limits

In the recent past, Congress would cast, on average, more than 500 votes per year (1,000 during a two-year session) on hundreds of bills. Although the number of bills has dropped some over time (e.g. 906 bills in 1948 versus 482 in 2006), the number of pages has gone up significantly (Beam 2009). It is estimated that Congress voted on 7,000 pages of legislation in 2006 alone. Budget bills frequently top 1,000 pages, and the Affordable Care Act was 2,000-plus pages at the time of the final vote.

Having so many bills—and especially bills that are long and complicated—is a boon for donors and lobbyists. Unless lawmakers serve on key committees that craft and vet a particular piece of legislation, it is highly unlikely that they will read it in its entirety. Instead, they will rely on staffers to read the bill and give them a concise summary/rundown of it; they will also depend on lobbyists to help them decipher what is in the legislation and how it will affect people.

There is great irony in the above arrangement: part of the reason why legislation is so long and complicated is because of the fact that lobbyists are inserting provisions into the bills. In other words, lawmakers rely on lobbyists to help them understand complex legislation—legislation that is complex precisely *because of* the lobbyists. It is a bizarre, twisted arrangement that should cease.

One way to stop this practice would be to limit the number of bills that Congress considers in a session; alternatively (or simultaneously), there could be limits placed on bill length. Either solution—especially in combination with single-issue legislation—could help end this odd relationship. But one more thing could help: forming a "congressional expert office" that could provide its own interpretation and assessment of legislation.

Congressional Expert Office

Lawmakers listen to lobbyists not *only* because of the money; they also listen to lobbyists because they view them as experts in a particular area. Say a bill comes to a lawmaker's desk that deals with auto emissions. They may seek out the help of a known and trusted donor/lobbyist from the auto industry to help them better understand the bill (assuming said donor/lobbyist isn't already offering their expertise). It makes sense on some level: the donor has been the lawmaker's friend over the years and has become a trusted source of funds *and* information. But there's no reason why others couldn't provide expertise of their own—and perhaps a different perspective—on legislation. In fact, we already have something like this with the Congressional Budget Office (CBO).

The CBO is staffed with experts in economics and accounting who look at proposed legislation and estimate how much it will cost over a certain period of time. The CBO is expressly nonpartisan—its job is simply to offer information and expertise related to the eventual cost of a bill. Why not expand beyond the CBO and have a complementary "congressional expert office" (CEO) that provides nonpartisan information on other aspects of legislation? It could be staffed by an assortment of highly-qualified experts from fields spanning the social sciences, arts, humanities, and natural/physical sciences. Its job would be to give an honest assessment of the impact of bills on society and the world. Its members could provide a much-needed alternative voice on issues so that donors and lobbyists are not the primary source of information for lawmakers. Besides, what politician wouldn't want to listen to a CEO?

106 *Political Reform*

Close the Revolving Door

As noted in Chapter 3, one of the benefits of campaign donations for politicians is the prospect of having a lucrative career as a lobbyist once out of politics. Although information on this practice is difficult to obtain given that most firms do not disclose their expenditures, a recent investigation into twelve lawmakers-turned-lobbyists found that they made millions of dollars as lobbyists, and their pay jumped an average of 1,452 percent (Fang 2012). It's little wonder that lobbying is the most popular post-Congress career for retiring lawmakers (Berman 2018).

One estimate suggests that nearly half—43 percent—of lawmakers who left office between 1998 and 2004 went on to become lobbyists (Berman 2018). This may not capture the entire number, however: many lawmakers do not officially become lobbyists, but, instead, *consult* for firms that engage in lobbying—or even take on top leadership positions in such firms. Sometimes referred to as "stealth lobbying" or "shadow lobbying," this kind of advocacy allows former politicians to engage in lobbying without being officially registered as lobbyists. According to a person interviewed by Berman (2018), "They organize the entire lobbying campaign, they identify who has to be contacted and what messages to say, and then they have someone else on the lobby team make the contact."

One example of stealth lobbying was already mentioned in Chapter 3: Tom Daschle went on to work for law firms and other entities shortly after losing his reelection bid. Although he was not officially listed as a "lobbyist," he consulted on issues that involved policy—and his status as a Senate leader very likely helped in that respect. Another example is Chris Dodd, who retired in 2011 after a thirty-year career in politics. Within weeks of retiring, Dodd became the President and CEO of the Motion Picture Association of America (MPAA), described as "Hollywood's lobbying arm" (Hiltzik 2015). There are numerous other examples—too many to fit in the pages of this book. The real question is how to curb this practice.

There are laws that restrict the lobbying activities of former politicians, but they clearly do not do enough to reduce this activity. Take, for example, the Honest Leadership and Open Government Act, passed into law in 2007. Among other things, the law prohibits former members of the House from engaging in lobbying for one year following their time in office (the limit is set to two years for former members of the Senate or the President's cabinet). Yet many former politicians are able to evade the rules through engaging in one of the many forms of "stealth lobbying" mentioned above. Moreover, even for those who follow the rules, virtually all of the limitations disappear after a year (or two), which allows former lawmakers to lobby as much as they want—and earn millions of dollars doing so—after the waiting period.

The laws on lobbying ought to be strengthened to close loopholes and make it more difficult for former politicians to engage in lobbying. At the very least, the waiting period should be more than a year or two; a decade would be far more appropriate. But this likely wouldn't be enough. Ideally, lobbying—in any form—would be banned entirely for former politicians. If this were to happen, the reciprocal exchanges between donors and politicians, discussed in Chapter 3, would likely diminish. After all, lawmakers appease donors not just because they are trying to return a favor—they also do it to stay on the good side of contributors. This serves two purposes: first, it increases the likelihood that contributions will keep coming from the target donors; second, it makes it more likely that the donors/firms would be open to hiring them after their time in office. If lawmakers are no longer looking toward lobbying firms for lucrative post-political jobs, some of the incentive to help donors would go away.

Reduce Conflicts of Interest

There are numerous conflicts of interest inherent in the way Congress operates today. There are three sources of conflicts, in particular, that stand out with respect to contributor influence: the makeup and funding of the FEC, politicians' ability to write their own rules, and the internal nature of so-called "ethics committees." Each of these will be addressed below.

Strengthen the Federal Election Commission

As noted in Chapter 2, the Federal Election Commission (FEC) is the entity tasked with monitoring campaign finance activity and pursuing cases in which there appears to be wrongdoing. The FEC faces a number of challenges, however, in conducting its work. Many of these difficulties arise from conflicts of interest related to how the FEC is composed and funded.

As mentioned briefly in Chapter 2, the FEC is a six-person body whose members are appointed by the President and confirmed by the Senate. This creates a conflict of interest, as politicians are

108   *Political Reform*

unlikely to appoint/confirm members who are strict on campaign finance issues. The FEC is funded by Congress. This again creates an obvious conflict of interest, as Congress can threaten to reduce the FECs funding if it is pursuing too many violations of campaign finance law. The end result of these conflicts of interest is that the FEC is mired in "dysfunction and deadlock" and does not do its job (Ravel 2017).

There are a number of reforms that could help the FEC function better and do its job. First, its members should no longer be appointed by the President and confirmed by the Senate. One proposal is to have the FEC populated by retired judges (Ackerman and Ayres 2004). Regardless of who they are, FEC commissioners should be individuals who are independent and willing to uphold the law. Second, the FEC's funding should not be decided by Congress. Instead, it could be set at a certain amount and then increased over time to adjust for inflation. Both of these reforms would help eliminate conflicts of interest and allow the FEC to actually do its job—monitor campaign finance and punish violators.

Forbid Politicians from Writing their Own Rules

Elected political actors effectively get to write their own rules. This is especially true of Congress given its lawmaking function. Being able to write their own rules presents a clear conflict of interest in that politicians can adjust policies in such a way that they permit themselves to do things that would simply not be allowed in other contexts. Take, for instance, the juxtaposition of the *Federal Bribery Statute* and current campaign finance laws, discussed elsewhere in the book. The *Federal Bribery Statute* clearly states that public officials cannot accept things of value in exchange for being influenced in official actions. Yet campaign contributions are of value to politicians, legislating is the official act of Congress, and research shows that contributions influence policymaking (e.g. Peoples 2010; Roscoe and Jenkins 2005; Stratmann 2005). So how are campaign contributions even permissible? Congress has allowed them via writing lax campaign finance laws, which are then interpreted favorably by the Supreme Court. In short, those who benefit from our open campaign finance system are the very individuals who wrote/approved the laws in the first place; as such, they have effectively made themselves exempt from the *Federal Bribery Statute* except for in the most egregious cases (e.g. making an explicit promise to do something in exchange for the contribution—a quid pro quo).

Politicians should be barred from making their own rules. Prohibiting politicians from making decisions on issues that affect them is not without precedent in the political world. For instance, judges are expected to recuse themselves from hearing cases in which they have a material interest in the outcome. Likewise, other political actors (e.g. lawmakers) are expected to do the same when deciding on policy that may have a financial impact on them or their family. These rules should be expanded to include policies that affect them in their respective roles. For instance, Congress should not be able to vote itself a pay raise. More importantly, it should not be allowed to exempt itself from the *Federal Bribery Statute* via campaign finance law.

Fortify Ethics Committees

Just as politicians get to write their own rules, they also get to police themselves via internal ethics committees. For example, the Committee on Ethics helps oversee ethics violations in the House—but this committee is made up of House members. Again, this represents an obvious conflict of interest. Allowing fellow politicians to decide whether or not they have broken the rules or deserve punishment is almost absurd. They are colleagues. They work together. They form bonds. They do one another favors. They even contribute money to one another via leadership PACs, as noted earlier. It's ludicrous that they would be the ones policing one another. Given all the aforementioned connections and dependent relationships between politicians, we cannot realistically expect that they would do a good job monitoring one another's activities and punishing infractions.

One potential solution would be to form independent ethics committees comprised of non-politicians. The challenge, though, is that this has been attempted already—and politicians keep trying to undercut them. For instance, the Office of Congressional Ethics (OCE) was formed in 2008. Less than ten years later, there was an attempt on the part of Congress to wrest away the OCE's independence and place it under congressional control. Thankfully, public outcry halted the move. But this effort on the part of Congress underscores the importance of protecting such entities from being undermined by the very bodies they are supposed to monitor. Much like with the FEC, their members should be independent and their funding should be linked with inflation. Further, ethics committees should be kept safe, free from meddling or closure on the part of politicians.

110   *Political Reform*

How Reform can Happen

So how can these reforms become reality? There are traditional avenues—Congress, the Supreme Court—as well as nontraditional approaches. All will be discussed below.

Congress

In the traditional avenue of Congress, attempts to reform our campaign finance system have had little luck. This is not surprising considering that those in a position to legislate reform (members of Congress) are also those who, arguably, have the least interest in such reform. Goidel et al. (1999) summarize some attempts, and failures, at reform in Congress through the 1980s and 1990s:

> A Republican-led filibuster in the Senate stopped campaign finance legislation in the 100th [1987–88] Congress. Although reform did pass the House and the Senate in the 101st [1989–90] and 103rd [1993–94] Congresses on party-line votes, differences could not be resolved in the conference committee.... More than ninety bills to reform the campaign finance system were introduced in the 104th [1995–96] Congress. None passed.
>
> (pp. 33–34)

There have been some more recent attempts to reform our campaign finance system. For instance, a "Democracy for All" Amendment was recently introduced as was the "Fair Elections Now" Act.

The Democracy for All Amendment sought to amend the constitution to reverse the *Citizens United* decision; the Fair Elections Now Act mandated, among other things, that congressional elections be small-dollar financed. Unfortunately, neither bill became law.

At the beginning of the 2019–20 Congress, democrats in the House introduced House Resolution 1 (HR1), which aims to reduce corruption and reform the campaign finance system. Although this resolution may meet the same fate as the earlier efforts mentioned above, it is not impossible for something like HR1 to pass.

As noted earlier, soft money reforms were finally passed in 2002 under the BCRA. Unfortunately, though, the reforms enacted in the BCRA were largely struck down by the *Citizens United* decision in 2010. This phenomenon of the Supreme Court rejecting campaign finance reforms is by no means new. But the Supreme Court has also indicated a willingness to uphold certain restrictions and consider factors such as corruption in its decisions.

The Supreme Court

The Supreme Court has heard a number of cases over the years related to campaign finance. Many of their decisions have served to weaken regulations and open the door to more contributions. In the words of Goidel at al. (1999:27), court decisions over the years have presented a major "impediment to comprehensive campaign regulation," leaving our present campaign finance laws quite weak. But the court's willingness to hear cases related to campaign finance indicates that they consider it an important matter that is not yet settled. Moreover, while they have indicated that "free speech" is a serious concern, they are willing to uphold certain restrictions when corruption—or the appearance of corruption—is involved.

Free Speech versus Corruption

In 1976, the *Buckley v. Valeo*, 424 U.S. 1, Supreme Court decision repealed certain existing campaign finance restrictions under concerns that said restrictions might limit the free speech of contributors. More recent Supreme Court decisions have supported the *Buckley* decision, and, in some cases, have weakened regulations further. For instance, as already noted elsewhere in the book, the *Citizens United* decision opened the floodgates to SuperPAC contributions— and the *McCutcheon* decision lifted overall limits on individual contributions—all in the name of "free speech."

One very important thing that should be mentioned about the *Buckley* decision and more recent opinions, though, is that they established *corruption* as a legitimate reason for limiting campaign contributions. For instance, while repealing some campaign finance restrictions, *Buckley* upheld some limits on contributions because of the "corruption or appearance of corruption" contributions entail, thereby establishing corruption as a key element (alongside "free speech") in deciding whether or not limits on contributions are constitutional. More recent decisions, such as the *Nixon v. Shrink*, 528 U.S. 377, decision in 2000, maintained this emphasis on corruption.

Sadly, though, the court has traditionally defined corruption narrowly as a quid pro quo market exchange, much like contributors and lawmakers do. For instance, the *McCormick v. United States*, 500 U.S. 257, decision in 1991 only considered contributions problematic if they "are made in return for an explicit promise or undertaking by the official to perform or not to perform an official act." Influence outside of this narrow definition is assumed to be benign—or is not

112   *Political Reform*

even viewed as influence at all. As noted in an earlier chapter, Justice Kennedy presented this argument the *McConnell v. Federal Election Commission*, 540 U.S. 93, decision.

But as has been illustrated in this book, the type of corruption described by members of the Court—characterized by quid pro quo, market exchange/bribery—is generally a rarity. Instead, institutional corruption—widespread exchange of gifts/favors among "friends" à la the social model—is the norm. Whether the Court would consider institutional corruption to be reason enough to decide in favor of reform is difficult to answer, but it is worth forwarding. As Lessig (2011) argues, "[Institutional corruption] is plainly corruption. It also plainly infects the political system for the same reasons that quid pro quo corruption does. In both cases, the consequence is to draw [lawmakers away from the factors they should be weighing in policymaking]" (p. 242).

Other Avenues of Reform

Congress and the Supreme Court are not the only potential avenues of reform—there may be other ways in which reform could be pursued. There are many ideas out there, but I will concisely describe three possible paths: state-level legislation, an Article V convention, and social movements.

State-Level Legislation

State governments have become more politically significant over the past few decades (Nathan 1993; Van Horn 1993). State governments often have greater flexibility in the policymaking realm, and, thus, they have increasingly become "laboratories of democracy" (Schultz 2002) where radical policy initiatives can be tested. Reflecting these realities, Van Horn (1993) notes that in the 1980s and 1990s, "the federal government often took a back seat to state governments in devising domestic policy innovations" (p. 7). This is true of campaign finance reform.

More than 50 percent of states have reformed their campaign finance laws since 1990 (Corrado and Ortiz 1997). Much of these reforms have entailed either limiting or eliminating private contributions. Describing recent state-level reforms, Corrado and Ortiz (1997:338) state that from 1980 to 1996, the number of states limiting PAC contributions had gone from sixteen to thirty-two. They also note that four states either established or tweaked already-existing public financing of campaigns, and a fifth state provided incentives for candidates to choose public financing (much like the policy at the federal level for presidential candidates, but with built-in perks for those who opt in).

State-level reforms are impactful in their own right (within their own states), but might also have the potential to reform things at the national level. In theory, a successful reform in a state might serve as a model for federal-level reform of our campaign finance system. Sadly, though, state-level innovations have not been immune to court scrutiny, and some of them have been struck down in the spirit of the *Buckley v. Valeo* decision. They are nonetheless worth trying. There are other options that are worth pursuing as well.

Article V Convention

Some argue that we ought to pursue an Article V convention. What is an Article V convention? It is a grassroots process, beginning in the states, in which Congress would "call 'a convention for proposing Amendments' to the Constitution if ⅔ of state legislatures ask it to…[and resulting Amendments] get ratified if ¾ of the states agree" (Lessig 2011:293). An Article V Convention carries the benefits of state-level origins but adds a layer of protection against judicial scrutiny. Anything coming out of an Article V Convention would not be struck down by a court, because, if successful, it would literally amend the Constitution.

An Article V Convention has only happened once in our history—when the framers used this process to create our Constitution—but it has come close to occurring numerous other times over the years. Importantly, each of these "close calls" has led to significant reforms (e.g. the Seventeenth Amendment) even without officially convening a convention (Lessig 2011:294)—so a push toward a convention may be enough in itself to bring about a Constitutional Amendment on campaign finance reform.

Social Movements

Both of the aforementioned avenues—state-level legislation or Article V conventions—could involve social movements as a grassroots element; alternatively, social movements could advocate for reform, more generally. Social movements involve groups of people working as a collective toward social or political change, using, at least to some degree, non-institutional tactics (e.g. protests, rallies, etc.).

114 *Political Reform*

Sometimes referred to as "unconventional politics," social movements exist in part because most regular folks do not have the same access to policymakers that the affluent do. In other words, social movements provide an alternative way for ordinary people—folks who do not have the resources to contribute to politicians or hire lobbying firms—to have their voices heard in Washington. How appropriate, then, that a social movement could be used to change the campaign finance system, thereby giving ordinary people more of a voice in politics.

Social movements have a rich history in the US, and have led to advances for many groups. For example, the labor movement ended child labor in the US and provided workers a forty-hour work week (as opposed to the eighty-plus hours that were common before the movement). The suffragist movement, as part of the larger women's rights movement, won women the right to vote. The Civil Rights Movement led to the Civil Rights Act and enforcement of desegregation in the US South. In short, social movements are an important force for change, and the same could be true when it comes to campaign finance reform. Indeed, this has already begun.

A social movement that dubs itself "Democracy Spring" has emerged to fight for campaign finance reform. Democracy Spring held demonstrations in Washington, D.C. in early 2016. Thousands of protesters converged on Washington to engage in the peaceful protests, and 900 were arrested (Golshan 2016). In addition to the protests, the Democracy Spring movement expressed support for two bills that would significantly alter the campaign finance system: the aforementioned "Democracy for All" Amendment and the "Fair Elections Now" Act.

Although neither bill became law, the mere fact that the bills were introduced speaks to the positive impact of the Democracy Spring movement. Hopefully the bills will be re-introduced in future sessions of Congress. Meanwhile, the Democracy Spring movement should continue to engage in activism and continue to pressure politicians to enact change.

Conclusions

Campaign contributions undermine our democracy, damage our economy, and increase inequality. Donations have corrupted our political system and have led to institutional corruption at some of the highest levels. Politicians are more responsive to their donors than to their constituents, and policy therefore reflects the wishes of the elite rather than the wants of the general public (Gilens and Page 2014). We have, in essence, become an oligarchy where a small percentage of wealthy individuals have sway in the political system at the expense of everyone else.

What are the costs of this arrangement for people in US society? The costs are great. Our current campaign finance system creates and exacerbates inequality—and can even lead to economic crisis. Through their impact on government contracts, subsidies, and the tax code, campaign contributions widen the gap between the rich and the poor. And through their influence on deregulation, campaign donations contributed greatly to the Financial Crisis and ensuing Great Recession. In short, campaign contributions are a danger to our society's institutions and our well-being, and should be greatly restricted—if not eliminated.

This chapter has offered numerous ideas of how we can reform our campaign finance system. It has also provided ideas for other reforms that might reduce the impact of campaign contributions. These ideas ought to be pursued for the sake of our society and its institutions. The time to act is now. Reform is desperately needed before contributions lead to another economic crisis or further undermine our democracy. The fate of our democratic republic hangs in the balance (Lessig 2011).

References

Abramoff, Jack. 2012. CBS News Interview. www.cbsnews.com/news/jack-abramoff-the-lobbyists-playbook-30-05-2012/3/

Ackerman, Bruce, and Ian Ayres. 2004. *Voting with Dollars: A New Paradigm for Campaign Finance.* New Haven, CT: Yale University Press.

Ansolabehere, Stephen, John M. de Figueiredo, and James M. Snyder, Jr. 2003. "Why Is There So Little Money in U.S. Politics?" *Journal of Economic Perspectives* 17:105–130.

Beam, Christopher. 2009. "Paper Weight: The Health Care Bill is More than 1,000 Pages. Is that a Lot?" *Slate.* www.slate.com/articles/news_and_politics/explainer/2009/08/paper_weight.html

Berman, Russell. 2018. "An Exodus from Congress Tests the Lure of Lobbying." *The Atlantic.* www.theatlantic.com/politics/archive/2018/05/lobbying-the-job-of-choice-for-retired-members-of-congress/558851/

Clawson, Dan, Alan Neustadtl, and Mark Weller. 1998. *Dollars and Votes: How Business Campaign Contributions Subvert Democracy.* Philadelphia: Temple University Press.

116 *Political Reform*

Corrado, Anthony, and Daniel R. Ortiz. 1997. "Recent Innovations." Pp. 335–392 in *Campaign Finance Reform: A Sourcebook*, edited by Anthony Corrado, Thomas E. Mann, Daniel R. Ortiz, Trevor Potter, and Frank J. Sarauf. Washington, D.C.: The Brookings Institution.

Fang, Lee. 2012. "When a Congressman Becomes a Lobbyist, He Gets a 1,452 Percent Raise (On Average)." *The Nation*. www.thenation.com/article/when-congressman-becomes-lobbyist-he-gets-1452-percent-raise-average/

Gilens, Martin, and Benjamin I. Page. 2014. "Testing Theories of American Politics: Elites, Interest Groups, and Average Citizens." *Perspectives on Politics* 12:564–581.

Goidel, Robert K., Donald A. Gross, and Todd G. Shields. 1999. *Money Matters: Consequences of Campaign Finance Reform in U.S. House Elections*. Lanham, MD: Rowman & Littlefield.

Golshan, Tara. 2016. "Democracy Spring: Why Thousands of Demonstrators Protested in Washington, DC." *Vox*. www.vox.com/2016/4/19/11457876/democracy-spring-demands-washington-dc

Hiltzik, Michael. 2015. "The Revolving Door Spins Faster: Ex-Congressmen Become 'Stealth Lobbyists.'" *Los Angeles Times*. www.latimes.com/business/hiltzik/la-fi-mh-the-revolving-door-20150106-column.html

Jones, Woodrow, Jr., and K. Robert Keiser. 1987. "Issue Visibility and the Effects of PAC Money." *Social Science Quarterly* 68:170–176.

Lessig, Lawrence. 2011. *Republic, Lost: How Money Corrupts Congress—and a Plan to Stop It*. New York: Twelve.

Mayer, William G. 2001. "Public Attitudes on Campaign Finance." Pp. 47–69 in *A User's Guide to Campaign Finance Reform*, edited by Gerald C. Lubenow. Lanham, MD: Rowman & Littlefield.

Nathan, Richard P. 1993. "The Role of the States in American Federalism." Pp. 15–29 in *The State of the States*, 2nd Ed., edited by Carl E. Van Horn. Washington, D.C.: Congressional Quarterly Press.

Peoples, Clayton D. 2010. "Contributor Influence in Congress: Social Ties and PAC Effects on U.S. House Policymaking." *The Sociological Quarterly* 51:649–677.

Ravel, Ann M. 2017. "Dysfunction and Deadlock: The Enforcement Crisis at the Federal Election Commission Reveals the Unlikelihood of Draining the Swamp." *Federal Election Commission*.

Roscoe, Douglas D., and Shannon Jenkins. 2005. "A Meta-Analysis of Campaign Contributions' Impact on Roll Call Voting." *Social Science Quarterly* 86:52–68.

Schultz, David. 2002. "Money, Politics, and Campaign Financing in the States." Pp. 3–26 in *Money, Politics, and Campaign Finance Reform Law in the States*, edited by David Schultz. Durham, NC: Carolina Academic Press.

Stratmann, Thomas. 2005. "Some Talk: Money in Politics. A (Partial) Review of the Literature." *Public Choice* 124:135–156.

Van Horn, Carl E. 1993. "The Quiet Revolution." Pp. 1–14 in *The State of the States*, 2nd Ed., edited by Carl E. Van Horn. Washington, D.C.: Congressional Quarterly Press.

Index

Note: Page numbers with "t" indicate tables and "f" indicate figures.

527 Groups 8; *see also* private campaign financing

Abramoff, Jack 74

Bipartisan Campaign Reform Act (2002): contribution limits by 8, 110; repealed by *Citizens United v. Federal Election Commission* (2010) 11, 16, 99, 111
bribery; *see* violations of campaign finance laws
Buckley v. Valeo (1976) 10, 111; *see also* First Amendment (Freedom of Speech)
Burstein, Paul 87

campaign finance laws: laws and contribution limits 11–16; history 9–11; *see also* violations of campaign finance laws
campaign funding system: institutional corruption 80; private contributions (*see* private campaign financing); public funding (*see* public campaign financing); reform of 4, 97–101
Center for Responsive Politics 25, 48, 50, 98
Cheney, Dick 60
Citizens United v. Federal Election Commission (2010): "Democracy for All Amendment" 110, 114; Free Speech argument 11; public opposition 11; BCRA repealed

by 11, 16, 99, 111; SuperPACs 1, 8, 16; *see also* Bipartisan Campaign Reform Act (2002); First Amendment (Freedom of Speech); SuperPACs
Cohen, Michael 73–74
Commodity Futures Modernization Act (CFMA) (2000); *see* economic implication of contribution
contribution—donor rewards: access to policymakers 20, 72; influence bill/law 20; influence policy decisions 20
contribution—electoral chances: private v. public funding 25; Electoral College point system 70; gerrymandering 70–71; incumbent advantage 23–24; "money primary" 24–25, 71; correlation 23–25, 71; voter-ID laws and disenfranchisement 70; winner-take-all system 70
contribution—impact on recipients: "leadership PACs" funding 25–26; connectedness and lobbying potential 26; electoral chances 20, 23–25, 36; income outside politics 26, 37; power/sway in political bodies 25–26, 37
contribution limits 11–12, 99–100; Bipartisan Campaign Reform Act (2002) 8, 11, 99; *Buckley v. Valeo* (1976) 10, 111, 113; Federal Election Campaign Act (1971)

118   *Index*

9–11; individual contributor 11, 100; PACs 11–12, 99–100; campaign finance reform 99–100; SuperPACs 12, 99–100
contribution pattern/trends: purposes 17; ideological strategy 14–17, 26, 92; individual donors 15–16; PAC contribution to federal elections (2000–2018) 14t; PACs (by type) 13–15; pragmatic strategy (bet hedging) 17, 23, 26, 92; SuperPACs 16; federal election spending (2000–2018) 13t
contribution—policy influence 27–37; statements/interviews 28; statistical evidence/studies 31–37
corruption; *see* violations of campaign finance laws
Cunningham, Randall "Duke" 59, 75–76, 75f, 82

Dahl, Robert 86–87
Daschle, Tom 26, 106
democracy implication of contributions: democracy v. autocracy/oligarchy 69–72; equal access to policymakers 4, 20, 72; free and fair elections 4, 70–71, 82; freedom of speech 4, 71–72, 82; public trust 2–3, 80; USA as oligarchy/plutocracy 69, 83; *see also* contribution and electoral chances; institutional corruption; organizational deviance; violations of campaign finance laws
DeVos, Betsy 29
direct ("hard money") contributions 8; *see also* private campaign financing; individual campaign contributions
Dodd, Chris 106
Domhoff, G. William 88

economic implication of contribution 41–51; CFMA (Commodity Futures Modernization Act) (2000) 41–42, 46–50; banking deregulation 46–48; campaign contribution to pass CFMA/GLBA (statistical proof) 48–51; Financial Crisis

(2007–2008) 42–45, 46–51; Glass-Steagall Act (1933) 46–48; GLBA (Gramm-Leach-Bliley Act) (1999) 41–42; The Great Recession (2008–2009) 45–46
exchange perspective 21–23; reciprocal exchange 22; illegality of negotiated exchanges (bribery) 23; negotiated v. reciprocal exchange 21–22; quid-pro-quo exchanges 76–77
expenditure limits; *see* contribution limits

Federal Election Campaign Act (1971) 9–11, 73
Federal Election Commission 10, 12, 98; function of 107–108; limitation through funding 12, 108; limitations through appointment procedure 12, 107; reform 108, 109
Financial Crisis (2007–2008); *see* economic implication of contribution
First Amendment (Freedom of Speech) 71–72; *Buckley v. Valeo* (1976) 10; contribution as free speech 102

Gramm-Leach-Bliley Act (GLBA) (1999); *see* economic implication of contribution
Great Recession (2008–2009); *see* economic implication of contribution

"hard money" donations; *see* private campaign financing
Hunter, Floyd 87–88, 90

individual campaign contributions 15–16; dominance of wealthy donors 15; ideological motivation 15–16
institutional corruption: politics as 79–80; definition of 79; legality of 76, 79–80; public trust 79; systematic, strategic influence 79; influence on government effectiveness 79

Index 119

Jefferson, William 76, 82

Koch brothers (Charles G. Koch and David H. Koch) 16

McCain, John 8, 25, 102
McCormick v. United States (1991) 76, 111
McCutcheon v. Federal Election Commission (2014) 11, 100, 111
Mills, C. Wright 88

organizational deviance: politics as 77–78; definition of 77; leader knowledge 78, 82; legality 77; socializing of new members 79; state crime as 80–81; state-corporate crime as 80–81; support within organization 78, 82; violations of external norms 77–78, 82

PACs (Political Action Committee) contributions 8–9; business PACs 13–14, 17, 23, 26, 36, 92–95, 97; contribution to federal election campaigns 14t–15t; dominant position of business PACs 14; ideological PACs 13–15, 17; labor PACs 13–14, 17, 36, 37, 92–95, 97; "leadership PACs" 25–26; lobbying firms 17, 29; statistical studies about 29–37; *see also* private campaign financing
political reform—campaign finance: anonymous contributions 100–101; "Grant and Franklin Project" 103; public campaign financing 101–103; Presidential Election Campaign Fund 102; "small dollar" campaign financing 100; contribution limits 98–99; transparency/disclosure 97–99
political reform—conflict of interests: self-legislation 108–109; independent ethic committees 109; Federal Election Commission 107–108
political reform—pathways: Article V convention (grassroot) 113; Congress 110–111; social

movement 113–114; state-level legislation 112–113; Supreme Court 111–112
political reform—policymaking 103–105; congressional expert office 105; bill size/number 104–105; single-issue legislation 104
political reform—restricting ex-policymaker lobbyism 106–107
Presidential Election Campaign Fund 7, 102–103; optional use 102; additional private contributions 2, 102; *see also* public campaign financing
private campaign financing 7–9; direct ("hard money") 8; history 9–11; indirect independent expenditure ("soft money") 8; *see also* PACs; SuperPACs; individual campaign contributions
public campaign financing: presidential elections 2, 7–8, 102; campaign finance reform 101–103; Presidential Election Campaign Fund 7, 102–103

research into contributions—political influence: business PACs 36; causality 33–34; evidence of PACs influence 31–37; low-visibility issues 33, 35, 37, 41; statistical studies (background) 29–30

"small dollar" campaign financing; *see* political reform—campaign finance
social inequality 52–66
social inequality—campaign contribution: government contract 59–60, 65–66; government subsidies 60–61; social mobility 57–58; Gini coefficient 54–55; government and wealth distribution 52; history 53–58; impact on individual lives 56–57; measuring inequality 53–55; policy focus on campaign donors 58; perceived degree of inequality 55–56; Tax

120 *Index*

Cut and Job Act (2017) 64–65; tax codes 61–65; tax reduction as contribution target 63–64, 65

"soft money" donations; *see* private campaign financing

state crime/state-corporate crime: socially injurious policy actions/ outcomes 81; definition of 80–81

SuperPACs (Political Action Committee) contributions 8–9, 16–17, 111; *Citizens United v. Federal Election Commission* (2010); ideological orientation 16; indirect independent expenditure (*see under* private campaign financing); freedom of contribution limits 1, 8, 11, 16, 99, 111; *Speechnow. org v. FEC—Citizens United* (Court of Appeals, 2010) 11

theories of power structure: case studies 90–91; elite power theory ("class dominance") 4, 87–88; empirical influence-outcome studies 91–94; pluralist theory (democratic ideal) 4, 86–87; state-centred theory ("institutionalism") 4, 89; US power structure as elite power/ class dominance 94–95

Traficant, James 75

Trump, Donald 29

violations of campaign finance laws 73–83; bribery 2, 59, 69, 72; bribery cases 74–77; corruption/ conspiracy 2, 69, 72; Federal Bribery Statue 23, 76; illegality of quid-pro-quo campaign contributions 77; legality of general campaign contributions 74–75; *see also* institutional corruption; organizational deviance